amigurumi
GOLF CLUB COVERS

25 Crochet Patterns for Animal Golf Club Covers

Linda Wright

Dedicated to my lifelong friend, Donna

Also by Linda Wright

Toilet Paper Origami
Amigurumi Christmas Ornaments
Amigurumi Toilet Paper Covers
Amigurumi Animal Hats Growing Up
Honey Bunny Amigurumi Dress-Up Doll
Honey Pie Amigurumi Dress-Up Doll
Chef Charlotte Amigurumi Dress-Up Doll
Summer and Sunny Amigurumi Dress-Up Dolls

Credits

Photography: Randy and Linda Wright

Acknowledgements

Special thanks to Anna for her keen eye, enthusiasm and support.

Edition 1.2

Lindaloo Enterprises
P.O. Box 90135
Santa Barbara, California 93190
United States
sales@lindaloo.com

ISBN: 978-1-937564-12-4
Library of Congress Control Number: 2018905654

Contents

Gopher
20

Pig
23

Alligator
26

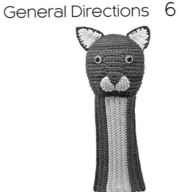

Tiger
29

Raccoon
33

Owl
36

Lion
39

King Cobra
42

Frog
45

Bald Eagle
47

Ladybug
50

Deer
53

Introduction

Welcome! I love designing functional amigurumi that will bring joy and whimsy to everyday activities. This collection of animal golf club covers includes 25 critters that would love to join you on the golf course and protect your clubs! You'll find a King Cobra, Gopher, Alligator, Labrador Retriever, Lion, Tiger, Bear, Bulldog, Bald Eagle, Tabby Cat, Penguin, Chicken, Flamingo and many more. The covers measure 14" x 6" x 6" which will fit up to a 460cc driver.

Amigurumi Golf Club Covers are quick and easy to make. These projects were designed to be simple enough that even a novice crocheter can complete the patterns with success. Before starting, be sure to read through all of the introductory pages where I've included lots of tips to help you along the way.

Amigurumi (ah·mee·goo·roo·mee) is a Japanese term for cute crocheted animals and objects. It is a colorful and cartoony style of stitchery that is so much fun. Most amigurumi is done by crocheting in a continuous spiral using one primary stitch—the single crochet—which makes it easy to master. Single crochet is also a tight stitch that works up into a thick fabric that is perfect for golf club covers.

Besides their cuteness, these patterns feature a padded lining made from foam stabilizer. This provides lovely structure for the head cover and an extra layer of protection for the clubs. Sew-in foam stabilizers for crafters are readily available and easy to use. They can be sewn by hand or with a sewing machine.

Each golf club cover has 2 primary parts: the Head Cover and the Ribbing. The Head Cover is crocheted in the round with 2 strands of yarn held together. The Ribbing is worked with a single strand and a smaller hook. The facial features are crocheted separately and everything is sewn together at the time of assembly. The assembly stage of amigurumi is always a thrill as you watch your animal come to life! Whether you're making these golf club covers for yourself or to give as gifts, they are guaranteed to bring smiles and cheer to all who cross their path.

For more fun and functional amigurumi, check out my other books: *Amigurumi Animal Hats*, *Amigurumi Animal Hats Growing Up* and *Amigurumi Toilet Paper Covers*!

~ Linda

General Directions

If you're new to crocheting, or if you need to brush up, the following pages include instructional photos for the stitches used in this book. If you like to learn by watching, YouTube. com offers a treasure trove of excellent video tutorials. To find what you need, just search on the stitch you want to learn. For example, magic ring crochet (also known as the magic circle or magic loop), chain stitch, single crochet, single crochet decrease or slip stitch. For a hand-picked source of tutorials, I have assembled a collection of my favorite videos on Pinterest. You can view them at www.pinterest.com/LindalooEnt/ on a board named "Amigurumi Tutorials". There you can watch demonstrations for all of the stitches and techniques needed for these projects.

In these patterns, you will sometimes be working with two strands of yarn held together. The multiple strands have the effect of a bulky yarn which makes a nice, substantial head cover. If you've never crocheted with multiple strands, just pretend you are working with a single strand and make each stitch as if you were holding one strand of yarn. That's really all there is to it. The ribbing and some of the auxiliary pieces are made with a single strand, so watch for that instruction at the start of each component. Also, watch for the hook size because it will change at times.

Amigurumi is meant to be crocheted rather tightly. This will prevent fiberfill from showing through your stitches on any stuffed pieces. Be sure to check your gauge.

The ribbing portion of each golf club cover is 8" long to protect the shaft. If more or less length is desired, simply adjust the starting chain for your ribbing.

It is standard procedure in amigurumi to leave long tails of yarn when you fasten off. These tails, or sewing thread, can be used when it comes time to sew all of the pieces of your golf club cover together. I use invisible sewing thread most of the time because it is so beautifully discreet, especially when sewing pieces of different colors together.

This book uses U.S. crochet terms. If an instruction says sc, that is a U.S. single crochet—or a U.K. double crochet. Please refer to the stitch diagrams on the following pages to be sure you are making the stitches as intended.

Yarn

These golf club covers were made with soft worsted-weight yarn marked as Number 4. This is a medium weight yarn. Look on the label for the yarn weight symbol  containing a "4" in the middle of a ball of yarn. For the best results, use the Suggested Yarns listed at the back of the book. Be aware that your yarn selection will affect your gauge because yarn thickness varies even within the Number 4 worsted category. The yarns that I used for these golf club covers lean toward the thinner side among worsteds. I primarily used Lion Brand "Heartland" yarn. This yarn is readily available for me and the colors are ideally suited for the projects. I also love that these are heathered yarns which create complexity in the colors and a multi-dimensional look. When I can't find a color that I want in the Heartland collection, other yarns that I typically choose are Red Heart "Soft" and Caron "Simply Soft".

Crochet Hook

The J10/6mm and H8/5mm hooks are used to make these projects and occasionally the G6/4mm. You may need to go up or down a hook size to obtain the gauge. My favorite hook is the Clover Soft Touch (below, center). I love the grip and the shape of the head which inserts easily into a stitch.

Yarn Needle

You will need a large-eyed needle to sew the various pieces of your golf club cover together and also to finish it off by weaving the loose ends into your work. Yarn needles with a blunt point are readily available. These will do the job though the blunt point tends to catch on the yarn and require some wiggling to push it through. I much prefer a needle with a sharp point. My favorite needle for sewing amigurumi is the Size 14 Chenille or Embroidery needle (see actual size photo below). These needles can be hard to find in stores, but they are available for purchase online.

Sewing Needle & Thread

Sewing thread can be used rather than yarn for sewing the pieces of your amigurumi together. The choice is mostly a matter of personal preference. I usually use thread for my golf club covers because it makes the stitches more discreet. If you don't have a thread stash, "Invisible Thread" will work for everything. This nylon or polyester thread comes in 2 colors: smoke and clear. Smoke blends with darker colors and clear with lighter ones. Invisible thread is a bit unruly to work with, but the results are worth the effort. For times when two contrasting colors meet, such as a Head Cover and Ribbing in different colors, it is perfect. If you have trouble threading a needle with invisible thread, color the end of your strand with a permanent felt tip marker. See Page 14 for how to attach sewing thread to crocheted fabric.

Scissors

You will need a small pair of sharp scissors.

Stitch Markers

Stitch markers are used to keep track of where a round or row of crochet begins and ends. You can use a safety pin, bobby pin, paper clip or purchased stitch markers. I like the locking stitch markers that are shaped like safety pins. They are very secure and easy to use. Making the correct number of stitches is important, so count to double check if ever you're not sure.

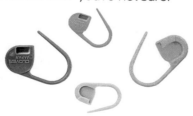

Animal Eyes & Noses

Plastic animal eyes and noses work magic in bringing personality to these golf club covers. They can be purchased at craft stores or online. A list of internet sources is included in the Resources section at the back of the book. One of my favorite sources, CR's Crafts, sells single sets in custom colors which makes it very economical to get just what you need. Standard animal eyes have a circular pupil while cat eyes have a slit-shaped pupil. Each eye consists of a post section and a washer. To attach, work post into a gap between stitches. Place washer against post, lay eye on a hard surface and press washer firmly.

Another way to attach animal eyes is with hot glue. In this case, cut the post off of the eye with wire cutters. Set eye in position and mark with an outline of 4 straight pins. Apply glue to fabric and put eye in place. (Read "Hot Glue Gun" section for further instructions.)

Note: Your club cover's lining will prevent the post from scratching a golf club. If you should choose to omit the foam lining, be sure to use the glue method of eye attachment.

Wire Cutters

To clip excess post off of animal eyes.

Hot Glue Gun

A high temperature hot glue gun can be used to attach animal eyes instead of using their posts and washers. When gluing, place a protective piece of non-stick aluminum foil behind the area to catch any glue that may drip between stitches. It's a good idea to practice with a spare eye on a scrap of crocheted fabric before gluing an eye to your golf club cover. Hot glue makes a very permanent bond!

Disappearing Ink Marking Pen

This terrific marking tool is helpful for marking the placement of snouts, beaks, etc.

Straight Pins

Use standard dressmaker's pins or long corsage pins to hold pieces in place before sewing.

Ruler

For measuring and marking.

Row Counter

Well worth the investment, a row counter keeps track of what round or row of the pattern you are crocheting. A pencil and paper can also be used.

Removable Notes

Use small sticky notes to keep track of your place in a pattern. Every time you complete a round or a row, move the note down to reveal the next line of instructions. I wouldn't work without one!

Stuffing

There are stuffed pieces in these patterns. Polyester fiberfill is my favorite stuffing material. This can be purchased by the bag at craft stores. One bag will go a long way! Scraps of yarn can also be used for stuffing small pieces.

Foam Stabilizer

A light-weight sew-in stabilizer consisting of a layer of foam sandwiched between 2 layers of soft fabric is used as the finishing touch and crowning glory for amigurumi golf club covers. This adds shape and body—plus additional protection for the clubs. Several brands are Pellon Flex-Foam, ByAnnie's Soft and Stable, and Bosal In-R-Form. You can sew them by hand or with a sewing machine. Some foam stabilizers are fusible, so be sure to get the sew-in type. Pellon Flex-Foam is the thickest for the most plush golf club cover. ByAnnie's Soft and Stable comes in white or black..

Sewing Machine

This is nice for assembling the lining, but not necessary. Hand-sewing also works fine.

Styrofoam Ball

A holder is handy when it comes time to pin a critter's auxiliary features in place. You can make one with a 4" styrofoam ball that is packaged in cellophane. (Keep the ball wrapped in its cellophane so it will slide over the crocheted fabric.) Insert one end of a dowel in the ball and the other end in a wood block drilled with a hole to match the dowel. Otherwise, a large goblet can be used or, of course, you can slide your cover on a golf club for your fittings.

Crochet Stitches

SLIP KNOT

This is used to make a starting loop on the crochet hook.

1. Make a loop about 5 inches from end of yarn. Insert hook in loop and hook onto supply yarn (yarn coming from ball) at A.

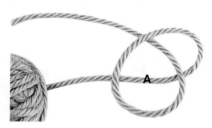

2. Pull yarn through loop.

3. Pull yarn ends to tighten loop around hook.

CHAIN (CH)

Start with a slip knot on hook.

1. Bring yarn **over** hook from back to front. Catch yarn with hook and pull it through the loop —

to look like this. One ch is done.

SINGLE CROCHET (SC)

This simple stitch is the primary stitch for amigurumi.

1. Insert hook in designated stitch. Note: Put hook under **both loops** that form v-shape at top of stitch unless otherwise instructed.

2. Yarn over and pull through the stitch (A).

You now have 2 loops on the hook:

3. Yarn over and pull through both loops on hook.

4. You now have 1 loop on hook and the sc stitch is done.

SINGLE CROCHET DECREASE (SC2TOG)

The instruction "sc2tog" means to use single crochet to join 2 stitches together. It is a way to decrease or make the item smaller.

1. Insert hook in stitch, yarn over and pull up a loop — to look like this:

2. Insert hook in next stitch, yarn over and pull up a loop — to look like this:

3. Yarn over and pull through all 3 loops on hook — to look like this. The sc2tog is done.

SLIP STITCH (SL ST)

1. Insert hook in stitch. Yarn over and pull through stitch and through loop on hook (A and B).

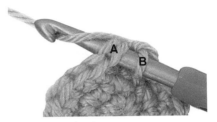

2. The sl st is done.

Techniques

★ MAGIC RING

Most all of my amigurumi begins with the magic ring. This is an adjustable loop that makes a neat center when crocheting in the round. If you're not familiar with it, you may want to watch a YouTube tutorial (see Page 99). It's not difficult — and well worth it.

An alternative to the magic ring, if desired, is to chain 2: then begin Round 1 by working the required number of stitches, as stated in the pattern, into the 2nd chain from the hook. This method will leave a small hole in the middle of the first round.

Make the Magic Ring as follows:

1. Make a ring a few inches from end of yarn. Grasp ring between thumb and index finger where the join makes an X. Insert hook in ring, hook onto supply yarn at Y and pull up a loop...

...to look like this.

2. Chain 1...

...to look like this. This chain does not count as a stitch.

3. Insert hook into ring so you're crocheting over ring and yarn tail. Pull up a loop to begin your first single crochet...

...and complete the single crochet.

4. Continue to crochet over ring and yarn tail for the specified number of single crochets for the 1st round.

5. Pull tail to close up ring. To begin the 2nd round, insert hook in 1st stitch of 1st round (see arrow).

BEGIN 2ND RND HERE

WORKING IN THE ROUND

Working in the round means crocheting in a continuous spiral. Most amigurumi is worked in this manner.

WORKING IN ROWS

Rows are worked from right to left. When you come to the end of a row, the instructions will tell you to turn. Simply rotate your crochet piece halfway around, in the direction that you would turn the page of a book, so that the last stitch you worked now becomes the first stitch you will work into for the next row.

USING STITCH MARKERS

It can be tricky to keep track of your place when working in the round, so be sure to use a stitch marker. The pattern will remind you! Place the stitch marker in the first stitch of a round — after completing the stitch. When you've crocheted all the way around, remove the stitch marker, make the next stitch, and replace the marker in the stitch just made. This will be the first stitch of the next round.

WORKING IN LOOPS

When a single crochet stitch is made, you will see 2 loops in a v-shape at the top of the stitch. To crochet the patterns in this book, insert your hook under **both loops** unless instructed otherwise. Crocheting in the "front loops only" or the "back loops only" is sometimes used for a different effect.

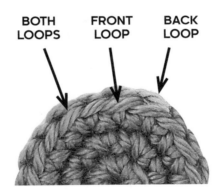

BOTH LOOPS   FRONT LOOP   BACK LOOP

CHANGING COLORS

To change color while single crocheting, work last stitch of old color to last yarn over, yarn over with new color and pull through both loops to complete the stitch.

FASTENING OFF

This is the way to finish a piece so that it won't unravel. When you're done crocheting, cut the yarn and leave a long tail*. Wrap the tail over your hook and pull it all the way through the last loop left on your hook. Pull the tail tight and it will make a knot. *Note: It is standard procedure in amigurumi to leave a generous length of yarn for your tail to use, if needed, for sewing your finished pieces together. In some cases you may prefer to use sewing thread for the final assembly to keep the stitches more hidden.

SMOOTHING THE EDGE

When fastening off, the knot can make a small bump in the edge of your work so that, for example, a round shape will not look as round as it should. To make the edge smooth, thread the long tail in a yarn needle and insert the needle down through the center "V" of the next stitch. This little step makes a big difference!

LARK'S HEAD KNOT

1. Follow pattern instructions for length and quantity of yarn strands to be used. Put hook through desired stitch, catch strand(s) in the middle and pull part way through stitch to make a loop. (Photos below show knot being made with 2 yarn strands.)

2. With hook in loop, lay yarn ends over hook.

3. Pull yarn ends all the way through loop. Take hold of ends and pull tight.

COUNTING ROUNDS

Periodically, it is good to count your rounds to ensure your place in a pattern. Fortunately, rounds are clearly defined and counting is easy. Each round makes a ridge. A groove separates the rounds. You need only to count the ridges. Take a look at the photo below to see that the circle has 5 rounds.

ASSEMBLING

The assembly stage of amigurumi is an exciting time for this is when all pieces are sewn together and the project blossoms in cuteness! It's a good idea to pin your pieces in place before sewing. Refer to each pattern's photo of the completed golf club cover for the placement of features. A rule of thumb is that the eyes are attached halfway up the animal's head or very slightly higher. For sewing, you can use the yarn tail of your feature piece or a sewing needle and thread. I tend to use a needle and invisible thread most of the time. When a small piece calls for stuffing, it's easiest to sew first, and when you have only a bit of space remaining to be sewn, pause and push the stuffing into place with your finger or the eraser end of a new pencil. Then resume sewing the final stitches.

ATTACHING THREAD

Sewing thread, especially invisible thread, is perfect for discreet stitches when sewing your amigurumi pieces together. To get started securely, follow the following steps:

1. Push thread through eye of needle and pull tail until the ends meet. Knot ends together to form a double thread (see A below).

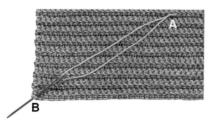

2. Run needle under a stitch at your starting point (see B above).

3. Run needle back between the 2 strands of thread and pull tight.

4. Done! Your thread has formed a secure Lark's Head Knot over the yarn.

WEAVING IN ENDS

Every pattern includes the instruction to "weave in yarn ends". This is the way to hide and secure all of your straggly yarn tails. Thread the yarn end into a yarn needle, then skim through the back of the stitches on the wrong side of your work. Continue for about 2 inches, then turn and double back to lock the yarn into place. Trim the end close. When you turn your work to the right side, you should not see the woven ends. They should be tucked into the middle of your crocheted fabric.

ATTACHING WITH SC

To attach yarn with single crochet, put yarn on your hook with a Slip Knot. Insert your hook into the indicated stitch on your crocheted fabric. Complete the sc as shown in Single Crochet tutorial, Page 10, Steps 2-4.

FRENCH KNOT

Bring needle up from wrong side at A. Place needle close to fabric and wrap yarn around needle 2 or 3 times. Push needle down at a point near A.

RUNNING STITCH

The Running Stitch is formed by a detached series of Straight Stitches. Make it by running the needle up and down the fabric at a regular distance. Come up at A, down at B, up at C, down at D, up at E, down at F, etc.

A B C D E F

LINING

Using the pattern on Page 97, cut 6 pieces from sew-in foam stabilizer (see Page 9).

- You can sew by hand using a Running Stitch (see Page 15) or with a sewing machine. If you sew by hand, pull your stitches tight enough to compress the foam.

- Allow 1/4" seam allowance.

- All seams are stitched with right sides together.

1. Sew 2 lining sections together (see Figure A).

FIGURE A

2. Sew on the 3rd lining section (see Figure B). Set this aside and sew the remaining 3 sections together the same way. When you are finished, you will have 2 halves of your lining.

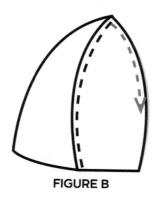

FIGURE B

3. Pin the 2 halves together with all edges even and sew together (see Figure C).

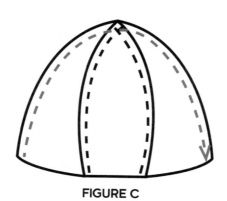

FIGURE C

4. Finished.

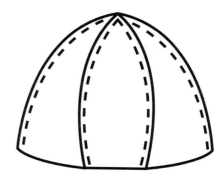

5. Turn right side out.

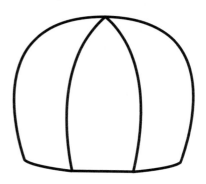

6. Insert Lining in Head Cover so that **right side of Lining faces wrong side of Head Cover**. This placement will give the smoothest appearance to your animal head. Roll up Ribbing so that you can see Lining edge. Adjust so that lower edge of Lining meets junction of Head Cover and Ribbing. With invisible thread and whip stitch, sew thru all layers around lower edge of Lining to secure it in place.

Abbreviations

Crochet patterns are written using abbreviations that save space and make the patterns easier to read. The following abbreviations are used:

st	stitch
ch	chain
sc	single crochet
sl st	slip stitch
rnd	round
sc2tog	single crochet decrease
yd	yard
* *	a set of sts
( )	stitch count

How to Measure your Gauge

Be sure to check your gauge when you start a pattern. This will ensure that your golf club cover is sized as intended and that the lining will fit. To alter your gauge, adjust your crochet tension (tightness) or change to a larger or smaller crochet hook. It is very common for gauge to vary from person to person. Yarn selection also affects gauge. Even within the worsted category, yarn thickness varies among brands and colors. For the best results, use the Suggested Yarns at the back of this book.

Gauge for the Head Cover:

With J10/6mm hook and 2 strands of yarn held together:

5 rnds of sc = 3" diameter circle

This means that when you've crocheted a 5-round flat circle of single crochet with 2 strands of yarn held together, the circle (or hexagon) you've created should have a 3" diameter. All of these Head Covers start with a flat circle made with 2 strands of yarn held together—so, when you have crocheted the first 5 rounds of a Head Cover, measure your work. If the measurement is 3", your gauge is correct.

Gauge for the Ribbing: With H8/5mm hook and a single strand of yarn, 15 rows of sc worked in back loops = 3"

When laying flat, a completed Head Cover should measure 6" vertical by 7" horizontal and the Ribbing should measure 8" vertical by 8.75" horizontal, as shown below:

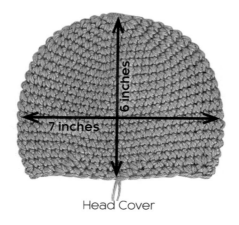

Head Cover

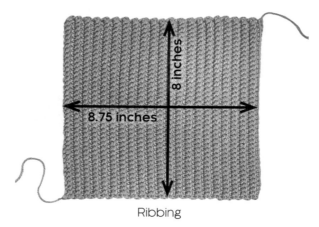

Ribbing

How to Read a Pattern

Each round or row is written on a new line. Most rounds have a repeated section of instructions that are written between two asterisks *like this*. The instruction between the asterisks is to be repeated as many times as indicated before you move on to the next step. At the end of a round, the total number of stitches to be made in that round is indicated in parentheses (like this).

Let's look at a round from a golf club cover:

Rnd 6: *sc in next 4 sts, 2 sc in next st* 6 times (36 sts).

This means:

Rnd 6	This is the 6th round of the pattern.
sc in next 4 sts	Make 1 single crochet stitch in each of the next 4 stitches
2 sc in next st	Make 2 single crochet stitches, both in the same stitch
6 times	Repeat everything between * and * 6 times.
(36 sts)	The round will have a total of 36 stitches.

So, following the instructions for Round 6, you will:

single crochet in the next 4 sts, 2 sc in the next st,
single crochet in the next 4 sts, 2 sc in the next st,
single crochet in the next 4 sts, 2 sc in the next st,
single crochet in the next 4 sts, 2 sc in the next st,
single crochet in the next 4 sts, 2 sc in the next st,
single crochet in the next 4 sts, 2 sc in the next st,

for a total of 36 stitches.

GOPHER

SUPPLIES

Worsted weight yarn in brown 135 yds; tan 105 yds; plus small amount of black and white

H8/5mm and J10/6mm crochet hooks or size needed to obtain gauge

Sew-in foam stabilizer, 10" x 20"

Invisible thread & sewing needle

2 white animal eyes, 18mm

Stitch marker

Yarn needle

GAUGE

Be sure to check your gauge (see Page 18) so that the cover is sized as intended and the lining fits.

HEAD COVER

With J10/6mm hook and 2 strands of brown yarn held together, make a magic ring, ch 1.

Rnd 1: 6 sc in ring, pull ring closed tight (6 sts).

Rnd 2: 2 sc in each st around. Place marker for beginning of rnd and move marker up as each rnd is completed (12 sts).

Rnd 3: *sc in next st, 2 sc in next st* 6 times (18 sts).

Rnd 4: *sc in next 2 sts, 2 sc in next st* 6 times (24 sts).

Rnd 5: *sc in next 3 sts, 2 sc in next st* 6 times (30 sts).

Rnd 6: *sc in next 4 sts, 2 sc in next st* 6 times (36 sts).

Rnd 7: *sc in next 5 sts, 2 sc in next st* 6 times (42 sts).

Rnd 8: *sc in next 6 sts, 2 sc in next st* 6 times (48 sts).

Rnd 9: sc in each st around.

Rnd 10: sc in next 17 sts, then work in back loops only (see Page 13) to sc in next 14 sts, then resume working in both loops to sc in next 17 sts; change to tan yarn in last st (48 sts).

Rnds 11-19: sc in each st around.

Rnd 20: *sc in next 6 sts, sc2tog* 6 times (42 sts).

Rnd 21: *sc in next 5 sts, sc2tog* 6 times (36 sts).

Rnd 22: *sc in next 4 sts, sc2tog* 6 times (30 sts).

Fasten off.

HAIR TRIANGLE

The hair triangle is worked in rows. The triangle is created by decreasing at the beginning and end of each row.

Use J10/6mm hook and 2 strands of brown yarn held together.

Note: A chain 1 at the beginning of a row is for turning your work and does not count as a stitch.

Row 1: refer to photo above and attach yarn with sc in first unworked front loop of Rnd 10 (counts as 1st st of Row 1), sc in next 13 sts (14 sts).

Row 2: ch 1, turn, sc2tog, sc in next 10 sts, sc2tog (12 sts).

Row 3: ch 1, turn, sc2tog, sc in next 8 sts, sc2tog (10 sts).

Row 4: ch 1, turn, sc2tog, sc in next 6 sts, sc2tog (8 sts).

Row 5: ch 1, turn, sc2tog, sc in next 4 sts, sc2tog (6 sts).

Row 6: ch 1, turn, sc2tog, sc in next 2 sts, sc2tog; change to black yarn in last st (4 sts).

Row 7: ch 1, turn, sc2tog twice (2 sts).

Row 8: ch 1, turn, sc2tog (1 st).

Fasten off. Weave in ends except black tail. Thread black tail onto yarn needle and make 1 stitch over Round 18. (See arrow below.) Teeth will be attached below this stitch. Weave in end.

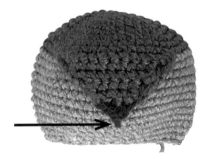

RIBBING

With H8/5mm crochet hook and a single strand of brown yarn, ch 41 loosely.

Note: A chain 1 at the beginning of a row is for turning your work and does not count as a stitch.

Work all rows in **back loops only** (see Page 13).

Row 1: sc in 2nd ch from hook and in each remaining ch across (40 sts).

Rows 2-17: ch 1, turn, sc in each st across; change to tan yarn in last st (40 sts).

Rows 18-25: ch 1, turn, sc in each st across; change to brown yarn in last st (40 sts).

Rows 26-42: ch 1, turn, sc in each st across (40 sts).

Do not fasten off. Pin last row and foundation ch row right sides together. Ch 1, sl st in each st across through both layers to form a tube. Fasten off.

EAR (MAKE 2)

With J10/6mm hook and 2 strands of brown yarn held together, make a magic ring, ch 1.

Rnd 1: 6 sc in ring, pull ring closed tight (6 sts).

Rnds 2-3: sc in each st around. Place marker for beginning of rnd and move marker up as each rnd is completed (6 sts).

Fasten off.

TEETH

With H8/5mm crochet hook and a single strand of white yarn, ch 5 loosely.

Row 1: sc in 2nd ch from hook and in each remaining ch across (4 sts).

Row 2: ch 5, turn, sc in 2nd ch from hook and in each remaining ch across (4 sts).

Fasten off.

ASSEMBLY

Stretch Ribbing open wide and insert Head Cover, right sides together, so that open edge of Head Cover meets an open end of Ribbing. Adjust so that center fronts meet. Pin in place, stretching Ribbing open and easing edge of Head Cover evenly around. Whip Stitch together with invisible thread. .

Attach animal eyes to Head Cover (see Page 8). Sew on Ears. Place Teeth in position and pull tails through to wrong side. Knot tails together. Sew a few stitches across top of Teeth with invisible thread.

Weave in yarn ends.

LINING

See Page 16 for how to make and attach the foam lining. This will provide structure for the Head Cover and more protection for the golf club. ♦

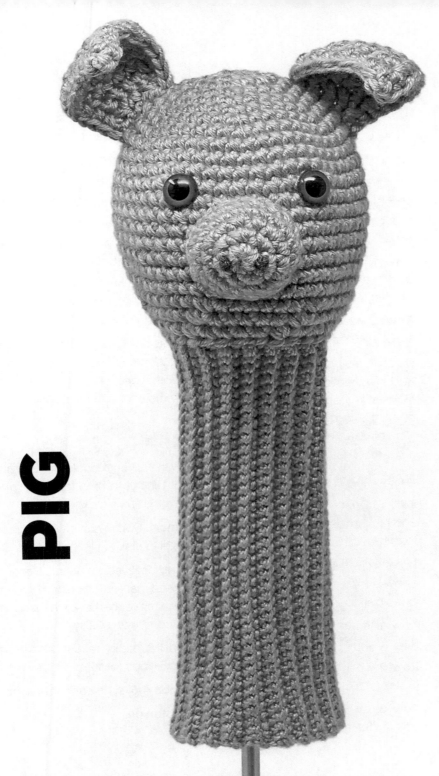

PIG

SUPPLIES

Worsted weight yarn in pink 270 yds; plus small amount of brown

H8/5mm and J10/6mm crochet hooks or size needed to obtain gauge

Sew-in foam stabilizer, 10" x 20"

Invisible thread & sewing needle

2 brown animal eyes, 18mm

Stitch marker

Yarn needle

Stuffing

GAUGE

Be sure to check your gauge (see Page 18) so that the cover is sized as intended and the lining fits.

HEAD COVER

With J10/6mm hook and 2 strands of pink yarn held together, make a magic ring, ch 1.

Rnd 1: 6 sc in ring, pull ring closed tight (6 sts).

Rnd 2: 2 sc in each st around. Place marker for beginning of rnd and move marker up as each rnd is completed (12 sts).

Rnd 3: *sc in next st, 2 sc in next st* 6 times (18 sts).

Rnd 4: *sc in next 2 sts, 2 sc in next st* 6 times (24 sts).

Rnd 5: *sc in next 3 sts, 2 sc in next st* 6 times (30 sts).

Rnd 6: *sc in next 4 sts, 2 sc in next st* 6 times (36 sts).

Rnd 7: *sc in next 5 sts, 2 sc in next st* 6 times (42 sts).

Rnd 8: *sc in next 6 sts, 2 sc in next st* 6 times (48 sts).

Rnds 9-19: sc in each st around.

Rnd 20: *sc in next 6 sts, sc2tog* 6 times (42 sts).

Rnd 21: *sc in next 5 sts, sc2tog* 6 times (36 sts).

Rnd 22: *sc in next 4 sts, sc2tog* 6 times (30 sts).

Fasten off.

RIBBING

With H8/5mm crochet hook and a single strand of pink yarn, ch 41 loosely.

Note: A chain 1 at the beginning of a row is for turning your work and does not count as a stitch.

Work all rows in **back loops only** (see Page 13).

Row 1: sc in 2nd ch from hook and in each remaining ch across (40 sts).

Rows 2-42: ch 1, turn, sc in each st across (40 sts).

Do not fasten off. Pin last row and foundation ch row right sides together. Ch 1, sl st in each st across through both layers to form a tube. Fasten off.

EAR (MAKE 2)

With J10/6mm) crochet hook and 2 strands of pink yarn held together, ch 2.

Note: A chain 1 at the beginning of a row is for turning your work and does not count as a stitch.

Row 1: sc in 2nd ch from hook (1 st).

Row 2: ch 1, turn, 3 sc in next st (3 sts).

Row 3: ch 1, turn, sc in each st across (3 sts).

Row 4: ch 1, turn, 2 sc in next st, sc in next st, 2 sc in next st (5 sts).

Row 5: ch 1, turn, 2 sc in next st, sc in next 3 sts, 2 sc in next st (7 sts).

Rows 6-8: ch 1, turn, sc in each st across (7 sts).

Row 9: ch 1, turn, sc2tog, sc in next 3 sts, sc2tog (5 sts).

Row 10: ch 1, turn, sc in each st across (5 sts).

Row 11: ch 1, turn, sc2tog, sc in next st, sc2tog (3 sts). This row is bottom of Ear.

Rnd 12: ch 1, do not turn, continue working forward and sc along both sides of Ear making 3 sts in same st at tip. Fasten off.

SNOUT

With J10/6mm hook and 2 strands of pink yarn held together, make a magic ring, ch 1.

Rnd 1: 6 sc in ring, pull ring closed tight (6 sts).

Rnd 2: 2 sc in each st around. Place marker for beginning of rnd and move marker up as each rnd is completed (12 sts).

Rnd 3: *sc in next st, 2 sc in next st* 6 times (18 sts).

Rnds 4-5: sc in each st around.

Fasten off.

ASSEMBLY

Stretch Ribbing open wide and insert Head Cover, right sides together, so that open edge of Head Cover meets an open end of Ribbing. Adjust so that center back of Head Cover meets seam of Ribbing. Pin in place, stretching Ribbing open and easing edge of Head Cover evenly around. Whip Stitch together with invisible thread.

Sew Ears on Head Cover. With brown yarn, make 2 French Knots on Snout for nostrils (see Page 15). Mark position of Snout with circle template (see Page 98). Stuff Snout and sew in place. Attach eyes (see Page 8).

Weave in yarn ends.

LINING

See Page 16 for how to make and attach the foam lining. This will provide structure for the Head Cover and more protection for the golf club. ♦

ALLIGATOR

SUPPLIES

Worsted weight yarn in green 385 yds and white 16 yds

H8/5mm and J10/6mm crochet hooks or size needed to obtain gauge

Sew-in foam stabilizer, 10" x 20"

Invisible thread & sewing needle

2 brown cat eyes, 24mm

2 black buttons, 3/8 inch

Stitch marker

Yarn needle

Stuffing

GAUGE

Be sure to check your gauge (see Page 18) so that the cover is sized as intended and the lining fits.

HEAD COVER

With J10/6mm hook and 2 strands of green yarn held together, make a magic ring, ch 1.

Rnd 1: 6 sc in ring, pull ring closed tight (6 sts).

Rnd 2: 2 sc in each st around. Place marker for beginning of rnd and move marker up as each rnd is completed (12 sts).

Rnds 3-4: sc in each st around.

Rnd 5: *sc in next st, 2 sc in next st* 6 times (18 sts).

Rnds 6-7: sc in each st around.

Rnd 8: *sc in next 2 sts, 2 sc in next st* 6 times (24 sts).

Rnds 9-10: sc in each st around.

Rnd 11: *sc in next 3 sts, 2 sc in next st* 6 times (30 sts).

Rnds 12-13: sc in each st around.

Rnd 14: *sc in next 4 sts, 2 sc in next st* 6 times (36 sts).

Rnds 15-16: sc in each st around.

Rnd 17: *sc in next 5 sts, 2 sc in next st* 6 times (42 sts).

Rnds 18-19: sc in each st around.

Rnd 20: *sc in next 6 sts, 2 sc in next st* 6 times (48 sts).

Rnds 21-44: sc in each st around.

Rnd 45: *sc in next 6 sts, sc2tog* 6 times (42 sts).

Rnd 46: *sc in next 5 sts, sc2tog* 6 times (36 sts).

Rnd 47: *sc in next 4 sts, sc2tog* 6 times (30 sts).

Fasten off.

RIBBING

With H8/5mm crochet hook and a single strand of green yarn, ch 41 loosely.

Note: A chain 1 at the beginning of a row is for turning your work and does not count as a stitch.

Work all rows in **back loops only** (see Page 13).

Row 1: sc in 2nd ch from hook and in each remaining ch across (40 sts).

Rows 2-42: ch 1, turn, sc in each st across (40 sts).

Do not fasten off. Pin last row and foundation ch row right sides together. Ch 1, sl st in each st across through both layers to form a tube. Fasten off.

OUTER EYE (MAKE 2)

With J10/6mm hook and 2 strands of green yarn held together, make a magic ring, ch 1.

Rnd 1: 6 sc in ring, pull ring closed tight (6 sts).

Rnd 2: 2 sc in each st around.

Place marker for beginning of rnd and move marker up as each rnd is completed (12 sts).

Rnd 3: *sc in next st, 2 sc in next st* 6 times (18 sts).

Rnds 4-7: sc in each st around.

Fasten off.

TOOTH (MAKE 8)

With H8/5mm hook and a single strand of white yarn, make a magic ring, ch 1.

Rnd 1: 5 sc in ring, pull ring closed tight (5 sts).

Rnd 2: sc in each st around. Place marker for beginning of rnd and move marker up as each rnd is completed (5 sts).

Rnd 3: sc in next 4 sts, 2 sc in next st (6 sts).

Rnd 4: sc in each st around.

Rnd 5: *sc in next 2 sts, 2 sc in next st* 2 times (8 sts).

Sl st in next st. Fasten off. Stuff yarn tails in tooth.

ASSEMBLY

Stretch Ribbing open wide and insert Head Cover, right sides together, so that open edge of Head Cover meets an open end of Ribbing. Adjust so that center

back of Head Cover meets seam of Ribbing. Pin in place, stretching Ribbing open and easing edge of Head Cover evenly around. Whip Stitch together with invisible thread.

Sew on Teeth with invisible thread. Sew on black buttons for nostrils. Fold tip of Head Cover forward so that tip covers Round 44. Sew a few stitches to hold in place. Attach cat eyes to Outer Eyes (see Page 8). Mark position for Outer Eyes with circle template (see Page 98). Stuff Outer Eyes and sew in place.

Weave in yarn ends.

LINING

See Page 16 for how to make and attach the foam lining. This will provide structure for the Head Cover and more protection for the golf club. ♦

TIGER

SUPPLIES

Worsted weight yarn in orange
    145 yds; black 60 yds; and
    white 25 yds

H8/5mm and J10/6mm crochet
    hooks or size needed to
    obtain gauge

Sew-in foam stabilizer, 10" x 20"

Invisible thread & sewing needle

2 yellow animal eyes, 18mm

Stitch marker

Yarn needle

GAUGE

Be sure to check your gauge (see
Page 18) so that the cover is sized
as intended and the lining fits.

HEAD COVER

Make Head Cover by alternating 3 rnds of orange yarn with 1 rnd, then 2 rnds, of black yarn throughout. (See color changes on project photo.) **Change to alternate color in last st of previous rnd.** For example, to work Rnd 4 in black, change to black yarn in last st of Rnd 3.

With J10/6mm hook and 2 strands of orange yarn held together, make a magic ring, ch 1.

Rnd 1: 6 sc in ring, pull ring closed tight (6 sts).

Rnd 2: 2 sc in each st around. Place marker for beginning of rnd and move marker up as each rnd is completed (12 sts).

Rnd 3: *sc in next st, 2 sc in next st* 6 times (18 sts).

Rnd 4: *sc in next 2 sts, 2 sc in next st* 6 times (24 sts).

Rnd 5: *sc in next 3 sts, 2 sc in next st* 6 times (30 sts).

Rnd 6: *sc in next 4 sts, 2 sc in next st* 6 times (36 sts).

Rnd 7: *sc in next 5 sts, 2 sc in next st* 6 times (42 sts).

Rnd 8: *sc in next 6 sts, 2 sc in next st* 6 times (48 sts).

Rnds 9-19: sc in each st around.

Rnd 20: *sc in next 6 sts, sc2tog* 6 times (42 sts).

Rnd 21: *sc in next 5 sts, sc2tog* 6 times (36 sts).

Rnd 22: *sc in next 4 sts, sc2tog* 6 times (30 sts).

Fasten off.

RIBBING

With H8/5mm crochet hook and a single strand of orange yarn, ch 41 loosely.

Note: A chain 1 at the beginning of a row is for turning your work and does not count as a stitch.

Work all rows in **back loops only** (see Page 13).

Row 1: sc in 2nd ch from hook and in each remaining ch across (40 sts).

Rows 2-4: ch 1, turn, sc in each st across; change to black yarn in last st (40 sts).

Row 5-6: ch 1, turn, sc in each st across; change to orange yarn in last st (40 sts).

Rows 7-10: ch 1, turn, sc in each st across; change to black yarn in last st (40 sts).

Rows 11-12: ch 1, turn, sc in each st across; change to orange yarn in last st (40 sts).

Rows 13-16: ch 1, turn, sc in each st across; change to white yarn in last st (40 sts).

Rows 17-24: ch 1, turn, sc in each st across; change to orange yarn in last st (40 sts).

Rows 25-28 : ch 1, turn, sc in each st across; change to black yarn in last st (40 sts).

Rows 29-30: ch 1, turn, sc in each st across; change to orange yarn in last st (40 sts).

Rows 31-34: ch 1, turn, sc in each st across; change to black yarn in last st (40 sts).

Rows 35-36: ch 1, turn, sc in each st across; change to orange yarn in last st (40 sts).

Rows 37-40: ch 1, turn, sc in each st across; change to black yarn in last st (40 sts).

Rows 41-42: ch 1, turn, sc in each st across (40 sts).

Do not fasten off. Pin last row and foundation ch row right sides together. Ch 1, sl st in each st across through both layers to form a tube. Fasten off. Weave in ends.

NOSE

With H8/5mm crochet hook and a single strand of orange yarn, ch 7 loosely.

Note: A chain 1 at the beginning of a row is for turning your work and does not count as a stitch.

Row 1: sc in 2nd ch from hook and in each remaining ch across (6 sts).

Rows 2-9: ch 1, turn, sc in each st across; change to black yarn in last st (6 sts).

Row 10: ch 1, turn, sc2tog, sc in next 2 sts, sc2tog (4 sts).

Row 11: ch 1, turn, sc2tog twice (2 sts).

Row 12: ch 1, turn, sc2tog (1 st).

Fasten off. Weave in ends except for black ending tail.

MUZZLE

With H8/5mm crochet hook and a single strand of white yarn, make a magic ring, ch 1.

Rnd 1: 6 sc in ring, pull ring closed tight (6 sts).

Rnd 2: 2 sc in each st around. Place marker for beginning of rnd and move marker up as each rnd is completed (12 sts).

Rnds 3-9: sc in each st around.

Rnd 10: sc2tog 6 times (6 sts).

Fasten off and thread tail onto yarn needle. Weave needle down through center of each stitch around opening. Pull tail tight to close hole. Weave in end.

EAR (MAKE 2)

With hook size H8/5mm and a single strand of orange yarn, chain 2 loosely.

Note: A chain 1 at the beginning of a row is for turning your work and does not count as a stitch.

Row 1: 3 sc in 2nd chain from hook (3 sts).

Row 2: ch 1, turn, 2 sc in next st, sc in next 2 sts (4 sts).

Row 3: ch 1, turn, 2 sc in next st, sc in next 3 sts (5 sts).

Row 4: ch 1, turn, 2 sc in next st, sc in next 4 sts (6 sts).

Row 5: ch 1, turn, 2 sc in next st, sc in next 5 sts (7 sts).

Row 6: ch 1, turn, 2 sc in next st, sc in next 6 sts (8 sts).

Row 7: ch 1, turn, 2 sc in next st, sc in next 7 sts (9 sts).

Fasten off. Trim tails to 1 1/2". Repeat with white yarn.

Place orange piece against white piece, wrong sides together, tucking yarn tails between layers.

Hold work white-side up. Using black yarn, fasten on with single crochet (see Page 15) at lower right corner (see Point A in photo). Single crochet around next 2 sides working each st through both ear pieces and making 3 sts

in same st at tip (see Point B in photo). Fasten off.

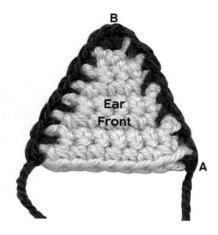

Ear Front

Ear Back

Sew lower edges together with invisible thread.

ASSEMBLY

Stretch Ribbing open wide and insert Head Cover, right sides together, so that open edge of Head Cover meets an open end of Ribbing. Adjust so that center back of Head Cover meets seam of Ribbing. Pin in place, stretching Ribbing open and easing edge of Head Cover evenly around. Whip Stitch together with invisible thread.

Thread yarn needle with black tail of Nose. Position tip of Nose at center of Muzzle and pin in place. Wrap black tail around lower half of Muzzle and push needle up from wrong side into black area of Nose, pulling tight. Sew up and down thru black tip of Nose and Muzzle to fasten them together. Sew Nose/Muzzle assembly to Head Cover with invisible thread. Attach animal eyes (see Page 8). Sew layers of Ear together along open edge with invisible thread. Sew Ears slightly cupped to Head Cover.

Weave in yarn ends.

LINING

See Page 16 for how to make and attach the foam lining. This will provide structure for the Head Cover and more protection for the golf club. ◆

RACCOON

SUPPLIES

Worsted weight yarn in gray 240 yds; white 25 yds; plus small amount of black

H8/5mm and J10/6mm crochet hooks or size needed to obtain gauge

Sew-in foam stabilizer, 10" x 20"

Invisible thread & sewing needle

2 white animal eyes, 18mm

Black triangle animal nose, 21mm

Stitch marker

Yarn needle

Stuffing

GAUGE

Be sure to check your gauge (see Page 18) so that the cover is sized as intended and the lining fits.

HEAD COVER

With J10/6mm hook and 2 strands of gray yarn held together, make a magic ring, ch 1.

Rnd 1: 6 sc in ring, pull ring closed tight (6 sts).

Rnd 2: 2 sc in each st around. Place marker for beginning of rnd and move marker up as each rnd is completed (12 sts).

Rnd 3: *sc in next st, 2 sc in next st* 6 times (18 sts).

Rnd 4: *sc in next 2 sts, 2 sc in next st* 6 times (24 sts).

Rnd 5: *sc in next 3 sts, 2 sc in next st* 6 times (30 sts).

Rnd 6: *sc in next 4 sts, 2 sc in next st* 6 times (36 sts).

Rnd 7: *sc in next 5 sts, 2 sc in next st* 6 times (42 sts).

Rnd 8: *sc in next 6 sts, 2 sc in next st* 6 times (48 sts).

Rnds 9-19: sc in each st around.

Rnd 20: *sc in next 6 sts, sc2tog* 6 times (42 sts).

Rnd 21: *sc in next 5 sts, sc2tog* 6 times (36 sts).

Rnd 22: *sc in next 4 sts, sc2tog* 6 times (30 sts).

Fasten off.

RIBBING

With H8/5mm crochet hook and a single strand of gray yarn, ch 41 loosely.

Note: A chain 1 at the beginning of a row is for turning your work and does not count as a stitch.

Work all rows in **back loops only** (see Page 13).

Row 1: sc in 2nd ch from hook and in each remaining ch across (40 sts).

Rows 2-42: ch 1, turn, sc in each st across (40 sts).

Do not fasten off. Pin last row and foundation ch row right sides together. Ch 1, sl st in each st across through both layers to form a tube. Fasten off.

EAR (MAKE 2)

With hook size H8/5mm and a single strand of gray yarn, chain 2 loosely.

Note: A chain 1 at the beginning of a row is for turning your work and does not count as a stitch.

Row 1: 3 sc in 2nd chain from hook (3 sts).

Row 2: ch 1, turn, 2 sc in next st, sc in next 2 sts (4 sts).

Row 3: ch 1, turn, 2 sc in next st, sc in next 3 sts (5 sts).

Row 4: ch 1, turn, 2 sc in next st, sc in next 4 sts (6 sts).

Row 5: ch 1, turn, 2 sc in next st, sc in next 5 sts (7 sts).

Row 6: ch 1, turn, 2 sc in next st, sc in next 6 sts (8 sts).

Row 7: ch 1, turn, 2 sc in next st, sc in next 7 sts (9 sts).

Fasten off. Trim tails to 1 1/2".

Repeat to make an identical piece. Place ear pieces wrong sides together, tucking yarn tails between layers.

Using white yarn, fasten on with single crochet (see Page 15) at lower right corner. Single crochet around next 2 sides working each st through both ear pieces and making 3 sts in same st at tip. Fasten off.

SNOUT

With J10/6mm hook and 2 strands of white yarn held together, make a magic ring, ch 1.

Rnd 1: 6 sc in ring, pull ring closed almost tight (6 sts).

Rnd 2: *sc in next st, 2 sc in next st* 3 times. Place marker for beginning of rnd and move marker up as each rnd is completed (9 sts).

Rnd 3: *sc in next 2 sts, 2 sc in next st* 3 times (12 sts).

Rnd 4: *sc in next 3 sts, 2 sc in next st* 3 times (15 sts).

Rnd 5: *sc in next 4 sts, 2 sc in next st* 3 times (18 sts).

Rnd 6: *sc in next 5 sts, 2 sc in next st* 3 times (21 sts).

Rnd 7: sc in each st around.

Sl st in next st. Fasten off.

OUTER EYE (MAKE 2)

With H8/5mm crochet hook and a single strand of black yarn, ch 13 loosely.

Note: A chain 1 at the beginning of a row is for turning your work and does not count as a stitch.

Row 1: sc in 2nd ch from hook and in each remaining ch across (12 sts).

Rows 2-8: ch 1, turn, sc in each st across; change to white yarn in last st (12 sts).

Row 9: ch 1, turn, sc in each st across. Fasten off. Weave in ends.

ASSEMBLY

Stretch Ribbing open wide and insert Head Cover, right sides together, so that open edge of Head Cover meets an open end of Ribbing. Adjust so that center back of Head Cover meets seam of Ribbing. Pin in place, stretching Ribbing open and easing edge of Head Cover evenly around. Whip Stitch together with invisible thread.

Sew Ears slightly cupped to Head Cover. Attach animal nose to tip of Snout. Mark position of Snout with circle template (see Page 98). Stuff Snout and sew in place. Attach animal eyes to Outer Eyes (see Page 8). Sew Outer Eyes to Head Cover.

Weave in yarn ends.

LINING

See Page 16 for how to make and attach the foam lining. This will provide structure for the Head Cover and more protection for the golf club. ◆

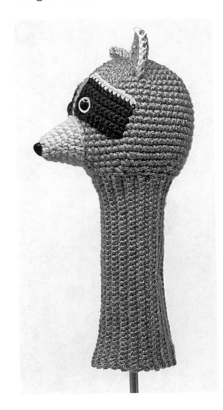

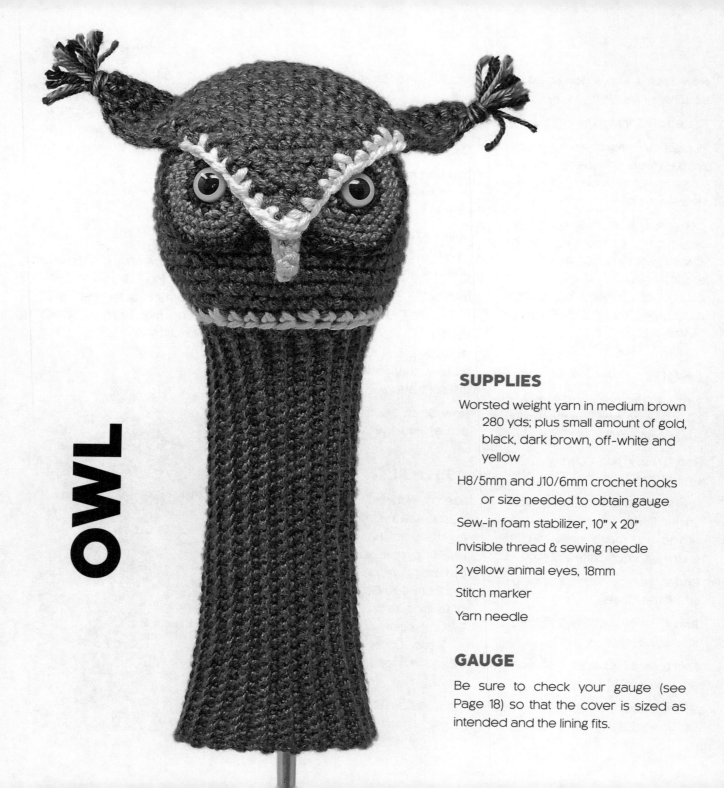

OWL

SUPPLIES

Worsted weight yarn in medium brown 280 yds; plus small amount of gold, black, dark brown, off-white and yellow

H8/5mm and J10/6mm crochet hooks or size needed to obtain gauge

Sew-in foam stabilizer, 10" x 20"

Invisible thread & sewing needle

2 yellow animal eyes, 18mm

Stitch marker

Yarn needle

GAUGE

Be sure to check your gauge (see Page 18) so that the cover is sized as intended and the lining fits.

HEAD COVER

With J10/6mm hook and 2 strands of medium brown yarn held together, make a magic ring, ch 1.

Rnd 1: 6 sc in ring, pull ring closed tight (6 sts).

Rnd 2: 2 sc in each st around. Place marker for beginning of rnd and move marker up as each rnd is completed (12 sts).

Rnd 3: *sc in next st, 2 sc in next st* 6 times (18 sts).

Rnd 4: *sc in next 2 sts, 2 sc in next st* 6 times (24 sts).

Rnd 5: *sc in next 3 sts, 2 sc in next st* 6 times (30 sts).

Rnd 6: *sc in next 4 sts, 2 sc in next st* 6 times (36 sts).

Rnd 7: *sc in next 5 sts, 2 sc in next st* 6 times (42 sts).

Rnd 8: *sc in next 6 sts, 2 sc in next st* 6 times (48 sts).

Rnds 9-19: sc in each st around.

Rnd 20: *sc in next 6 sts, sc2tog* 6 times (42 sts).

Rnd 21: *sc in next 5 sts, sc2tog* 6 times; change to off-white yarn in last st (36 sts).

Rnd 22: *sc in next 4 sts, sc2tog* 6 times (30 sts).

Fasten off.

RIBBING

With H8/5mm crochet hook and a single strand of medium brown yarn, ch 41 loosely.

Note: A chain 1 at the beginning of a row is for turning your work and does not count as a stitch.

Work all rows in **back loops only** (see Page 13).

Row 1: sc in 2nd ch from hook and in each remaining ch across (40 sts).

Rows 2-42: ch 1, turn, sc in each st across (40 sts).

Do not fasten off. Pin last row and foundation ch row right sides together. Ch 1, sl st in each st across through both layers to form a tube. Fasten off.

EYE RIM (MAKE 2)

With H8/5mm hook and a single strand of black yarn, make a magic ring, ch 1.

Rnd 1: 6 sc in ring, pull ring closed almost tight (6 sts).

Rnd 2: 2 sc in each st around; change to gold yarn in last st. Place marker for beginning of rnd and move marker up as each rnd is completed (12 sts).

Rnd 3: *sc in next st, 2 sc in next st* 6 times (18 sts).

Rnd 4: *sc in next 2 sts, 2 sc in next st* 6 times (24 sts).

Rnd 5: *sc in next 3 sts, 2 sc in next st* 6 times; change to dark brown yarn in last st (30 sts).

Rnd 6: *sc in next 4 sts, 2 sc in next st* 6 times (36 sts).

Sl st in next st. Fasten off.

TOP TRIANGLE

The triangle is created by decreasing at the beginning and end of each row.

With hook size J10/6mm and 2 strands of medium brown yarn held together, ch 29 loosely.

Note: A chain 1 at the beginning of a row is for turning your work and does not count as a stitch.

Row 1: starting in 2nd ch from hook, sc2tog, sc in each ch across until 2 ch remain, sc2tog.

Rows 2-end: ch 1, turn, sc2tog, sc in each st across until 2 sts remain, sc2tog. Continue working rows in this manner until 1 st remains. Fasten off.

With medium brown yarn and right side up, sc along Sides CB and BA, changing to off-white for 3" on each side of Point B.

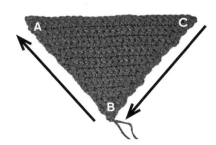

Leave yarn tails at Points A and C to be used in Tufts. Weave in all other loose ends.

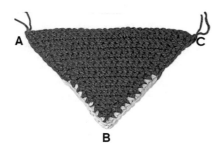

TUFT (MAKE 2)

Cut three 8-inch strands of gold and three 8-inch strands of dark brown yarn. Lay strands together and attach to Point A of Top Triangle using Lark's Head Knot (see Page 14). Trim to 1 inch. Repeat for Point C.

BEAK

With H8/5mm hook and a single strand of yellow yarn, make a magic ring, ch 1.

Rnd 1: 6 sc in ring, pull ring closed tight (6 sts).

Rnd 2: 2 sc in each st around. Place marker for beginning of rnd and move marker up as each rnd is completed (12 sts).

Rnd 3: *sc in next st, 2 sc in next st* 6 times (18 sts).

Fasten off.

With wrong side up, fold sides inward (see Y). Sew to hold in position (see Z).

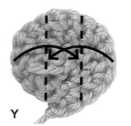

ASSEMBLY

Stretch Ribbing open wide and insert Head Cover, right sides together, so that open edge of Head Cover meets an open end of Ribbing. Adjust so that center back of Head Cover meets seam of Ribbing. Pin in place, stretching Ribbing open and easing edge of Head Cover evenly around. Whip Stitch together with invisible thread. Weave in yarn ends.

Attach eyes to center of Eye Rims (see Page 8). Clip off excess stem with wire cutters. Pin Eye Rims in place rotating them so that uneven jog of black in Rnd 2 (where color was changed) will be hidden by Top Triangle. Sew to Head Cover with invisible thread.

Sew on Beak.

Pin Top Triangle to Head Cover. Sew in place with invisible thread along the off-white edgestitching

and along a 4" section at center back. (See red lines below.) This will leave the corners free. Flip corners up.

LINING

See Page 16 for how to make and attach the foam lining. This will provide structure for the Head Cover and more protection for the golf club. ♦

LION

SUPPLIES

Worsted weight yarn in tan 310 yds; plus small amount of white and black

H8/5mm and J10/6mm crochet hooks or size needed to obtain gauge

Sew-in foam stabilizer, 10" x 20"

Invisible thread & sewing needle

2 gold animal eyes, 18mm

Stitch marker

Yarn needle

Small piece of cardboard

GAUGE

Be sure to check your gauge (see Page 18) so that the cover is sized as intended and the lining fits.

HEAD COVER

With J10/6mm hook and 2 strands of tan yarn held together, make a magic ring, ch 1.

Rnd 1: 6 sc in ring, pull ring closed tight (6 sts).

Rnd 2: 2 sc in each st around. Place marker for beginning of rnd and move marker up as each rnd is completed (12 sts).

Rnd 3: *sc in next st, 2 sc in next st* 6 times (18 sts).

Rnd 4: *sc in next 2 sts, 2 sc in next st* 6 times (24 sts).

Rnd 5: *sc in next 3 sts, 2 sc in next st* 6 times (30 sts).

Rnd 6: *sc in next 4 sts, 2 sc in next st* 6 times (36 sts).

Rnd 7: *sc in next 5 sts, 2 sc in next st* 6 times (42 sts).

Rnd 8: *sc in next 6 sts, 2 sc in next st* 6 times (48 sts).

Rnds 9-19: sc in each st around.

Rnd 20: *sc in next 6 sts, sc2tog* 6 times (42 sts).

Rnd 21: *sc in next 5 sts, sc2tog* 6 times (36 sts).

Rnd 22: *sc in next 4 sts, sc2tog* 6 times (30 sts).

Fasten off.

RIBBING

With H8/5mm crochet hook and a single strand of tan yarn, ch 41 loosely.

Note: A chain 1 at the beginning of a row is for turning your work and does not count as a stitch.

Work all rows in **back loops only** (see Page 13).

Row 1: sc in 2nd ch from hook and in each remaining ch across (40 sts).

Rows 2-42: ch 1, turn, sc in each st across (40 sts).

Do not fasten off. Pin last row and foundation ch row right sides together. Ch 1, sl st in each st across through both layers to form a tube. Fasten off.

EAR (MAKE 2)

With H8/5mm crochet hook and a single strand of tan yarn, make a magic ring, ch 1.

Rnd 1: 6 sc in ring, pull ring closed tight (6 sts).

Rnd 2: 2 sc in each st around. Place marker for beginning of rnd and move marker up as each rnd is completed (12 sts).

Rnd 3: *sc in next st, 2 sc in next st* 6 times (18 sts).

Rnds 4-9: sc in each st around.

Fasten off.

NOSE

With H8/5mm crochet hook and a single strand of tan yarn, ch 7 loosely.

Note: A chain 1 at the beginning of a row is for turning your work and does not count as a stitch.

Row 1: sc in 2nd ch from hook and in each remaining ch across (6 sts).

Rows 2-9: ch 1, turn, sc in each st across; change to black yarn in last st (6 sts).

Row 10: ch 1, turn, sc2tog, sc in next 2 sts, sc2tog (4 sts).

Row 11: ch 1, turn, sc2tog twice (2 sts).

Row 12: ch 1, turn, sc2tog (1 st).

Fasten off. Weave in ends except for black ending tail.

MUZZLE

With H8/5mm crochet hook and a single strand of white yarn, make a magic ring, ch 1.

Rnd 1: 6 sc in ring, pull ring closed tight (6 sts).

Rnd 2: 2 sc in each st around. Place marker for beginning of rnd and move marker up as each rnd is completed (12 sts).

Rnds 3-9: sc in each st around.

Rnd 10: sc2tog 6 times (6 sts).

Fasten off and thread tail onto yarn needle. Weave needle down through center of each stitch around opening. Pull tail tight to close hole. Weave in end.

ASSEMBLY

Stretch Ribbing open wide and insert Head Cover, right sides together, so that open edge of Head Cover meets an open end of Ribbing. Adjust so that center back of Head Cover meets seam of Ribbing. Pin in place, stretching Ribbing open and easing edge of Head Cover evenly around. Whip Stitch together with invisible thread. Weave in yarn ends.

For the mane, you will need many 6-inch pieces of tan yarn. To quickly cut the strands, wrap yarn widthwise around a 3" x 9" piece

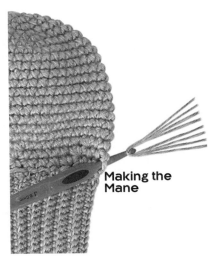

Making the Mane

of cardboard. On one side, insert scissors between cardboard and yarn—and cut.

Flatten Head Cover and finger press so that center front meets center back. Put hook through a st on crease and follow instructions for Lark's Head Knot (see Page 14) using **4 strands** of yarn. Repeat knot in each st around crease. (See Figure A.)

NOTE: When making fringe, the knots can face the front or back. In this case, I like them to face the back. This will push the fringe forward so that it frames the Lion's face nicely.

Fill in center-front hairline with 2 more rows of Lark's Head Knots in front of 1st row and fill in lower corners with several knots (see Figure A).

For the lower front (see red dots, Figure A), cut some longer 8-inch strands of yarn and insert in same manner. Trim lower front into a beard shape that blends into sides of mane. If you trim some of the top strands of the beard a bit shorter, it will create nice layers.

Sew Ears in place.

Thread needle with black tail of Nose. Position tip of Nose at center of Muzzle and pin in place. Wrap black tail around lower half of Muzzle and push needle up

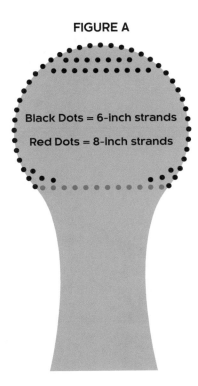

FIGURE A

Black Dots = 6-inch strands

Red Dots = 8-inch strands

from wrong side into black area of Nose, pulling tight. Sew up and down several times through Nose and Muzzle to fasten them together. Sew Nose/Muzzle assembly to Head Cover with invisible thread.

Attach animal eyes (see Page 8).

LINING

See Page 16 for how to make and attach the foam lining. This will provide structure for the Head Cover and more protection for the golf club. ◆

KING COBRA

SUPPLIES

Worsted weight yarn in brown 325 yds; tan 35 yds; plus small amount of pink and black

H8/5mm and J10/6mm crochet hooks or size needed to obtain gauge

Sew-in foam stabilizer, 10" x 20"

Invisible thread & sewing needle

2 yellow cat eyes, 15mm

Stitch marker

Yarn needle

GAUGE

Be sure to check your gauge (see Page 18) so that the cover is sized as intended and the lining fits.

TONGUE

With J10/6mm hook and 2 strands of pink yarn held together, ch 12. Fasten off.

Fasten on in 7th chain, ch 5. Fasten off.

With yarn needle, sew loose tails through stitches so that all tails exit at Point A.

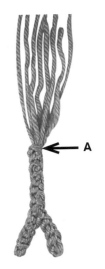

← A

HEAD COVER

With J10/6mm hook and 2 strands of brown yarn held together, make a magic ring, ch 1.

Rnd 1: 6 sc in ring, pull ring closed almost tight (6 sts).

Rnd 2: 2 sc in each st around. Place marker for beginning of rnd and move marker up as each rnd is completed (12 sts).

Attach Tongue: Pull Tongue tails through center of Rnd 1 to wrong side of work. Tie Tongue tails together with Head Cover tails and knot securely.

Rnds 3-4: sc in each st around.

Rnd 5: *sc in next st, 2 sc in next st* 6 times (18 sts).

Rnds 6-7: sc in each st around.

Rnd 8: *sc in next 2 sts, 2 sc in next st* 6 times (24 sts).

Rnds 9-10: sc in each st around.

Attach Eyes: Position eyes in groove between Rnds 7-8 and attach (see Page 8).

Rnd 11: *sc in next 3 sts, 2 sc in next st* 6 times (30 sts).

Rnds 12-13: sc in each st around.

Rnd 14: *sc in next 4 sts, 2 sc in next st* 6 times (36 sts).

Rnds 15-16: sc in each st around.

Rnd 17: *sc in next 5 sts, 2 sc in next st* 6 times (42 sts).

Rnds 18-19: sc in each st around.

Rnd 20: *sc in next 6 sts, 2 sc in next st* 6 times (48 sts).

Rnds 21-40: sc in each st around.

Rnd 41: *sc in next 6 sts, sc2tog* 6 times (42 sts).

Rnd 42: *sc in next 5 sts, sc2tog* 6 times (36 sts).

Rnd 43: *sc in next 4 sts, sc2tog* 6 times (30 sts). Fasten off.

RIBBING

With H8/5mm crochet hook and a single strand of brown yarn, ch 41 loosely.

Note: A chain 1 at the beginning of a row is for turning your work and does not count as a stitch.

Work all rows in **back loops only** (see Page 13).

Row 1: sc in 2nd ch from hook and in each remaining ch across (40 sts).

Rows 2-42: ch 1, turn, sc in each st across (40 sts).

Do not fasten off. Pin last row and foundation ch row right sides together. Ch 1, sl st in each st across through both layers to form a tube. Fasten off.

BELLY STRIPE

With H8/5mm crochet hook and a single strand of tan yarn, ch 71 loosely.

Note: A chain 1 at the beginning of a row is for turning your work and does not count as a stitch.

Work all rows in **back loops only** (see Page 13).

Row 1: sc in 2nd ch from hook and in each remaining ch across (70 sts).

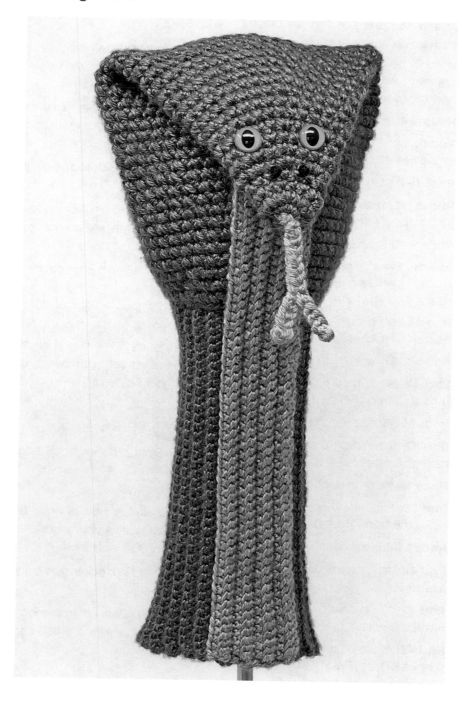

Rows 2-8: ch 1, turn, sc in each st across (70 sts).

Fasten off.

ASSEMBLY

Stretch Ribbing open wide and insert Head Cover, right sides together, so that open edge of Head Cover meets an open end of Ribbing. Adjust so that center back of Head Cover meets seam of Ribbing. Pin in place, stretching Ribbing open and easing edge of Head Cover evenly around. Whip Stitch together with invisible thread. Weave in yarn ends.

Pin Belly Stripe to center front with lower edges even. Sew in place with invisible thread.

Flatten tip of Head Cover and embroider, with a single strand of black yarn, French Knots for nostrils (see Page 15). Fold tip forward to meet Round 37 and sew a few stitches to hold in place.

LINING

See Page 16 for how to make and attach the foam lining. This will provide structure for the Head Cover and more protection for the golf club. ♦

FROG

SUPPLIES

Worsted weight yarn in green 260 yds; plus small amount of black

H8/5mm and J10/6mm crochet hooks or size needed to obtain gauge

Sew-in foam stabilizer, 10" x 20"

Invisible thread & sewing needle

2 white animal eyes, 24mm

Stitch marker

Yarn needle

Stuffing

GAUGE

Be sure to check your gauge (see Page 18) so that the cover is sized as intended and the lining fits.

HEAD COVER

With J10/6mm hook and 2 strands of green yarn held together, make a magic ring, ch 1.

Rnd 1: 6 sc in ring, pull ring closed tight (6 sts).

Rnd 2: 2 sc in each st around. Place marker for beginning of rnd and move marker up as each rnd is completed (12 sts).

Rnd 3: *sc in next st, 2 sc in next st* 6 times (18 sts).

Rnd 4: *sc in next 2 sts, 2 sc in next st* 6 times (24 sts).

Rnd 5: *sc in next 3 sts, 2 sc in next st* 6 times (30 sts).

Rnd 6: *sc in next 4 sts, 2 sc in next st* 6 times (36 sts).

Rnd 7: *sc in next 5 sts, 2 sc in next st* 6 times (42 sts).

Rnd 8: *sc in next 6 sts, 2 sc in next st* 6 times (48 sts).

Rnds 9-18: sc in each st around.

Rnd 19: sc in next 12 sts changing to black yarn in last st, sc in next 24 sts changing to green yarn in last st, sc in next 12 sts (48 sts).

Rnd 20: *sc in next 6 sts, sc2tog* 6 times (42 sts).

Rnd 21: *sc in next 5 sts, sc2tog* 6 times (36 sts).

Rnd 22: *sc in next 4 sts, sc2tog* 6 times (30 sts). Fasten off.

RIBBING

With H8/5mm crochet hook and a single strand of green yarn, ch 41 loosely.

Note: A chain 1 at the beginning of a row is for turning your work and does not count as a stitch.

Work all rows in **back loops only** (see Page 13).

Row 1: sc in 2nd ch from hook and in each remaining ch across (40 sts).

Rows 2-42: ch 1, turn, sc in each st across (40 sts).

Do not fasten off. Pin last row and foundation ch row right sides together. Ch 1, sl st in each st across through both layers to form a tube. Fasten off.

OUTER EYE (MAKE 2)

With H8/5mm hook and 2 strands of green yarn held together, make a magic ring, ch 1.

Rnd 1: 6 sc in ring, pull ring closed tight (6 sts).

Rnd 2: 2 sc in each st around. Place marker for beginning of rnd and move marker up as each rnd is completed (12 sts).

Rnd 3: *sc in next st, 2 sc in next st* 6 times (18 sts).

Rnd 4: *sc in next 2 sts, 2 sc in next st* 6 times (24 sts).

Rnds 5-9: sc in each st around.

Fasten off.

ASSEMBLY

With a double strand of black yarn, embroider 2 straight stitches on Head Cover for nostrils.

Stretch Ribbing open wide and insert Head Cover, right sides together, so that open edge of Head Cover meets an open end of Ribbing. Adjust so that center back of Head Cover meets seam of Ribbing. Pin in place, stretching Ribbing open and easing edge of Head Cover evenly around. Whip Stitch together with invisible thread. Weave in yarn ends.

Attach animal eyes to Outer Eyes (see Page 8). Mark position of Outer Eyes on Head Cover with circle template (see Page 98). Stuff Outer Eyes and sew in place.

LINING

See Page 16 for how to make and attach the foam lining. This will provide structure for the Head Cover and more protection for the golf club. ♦

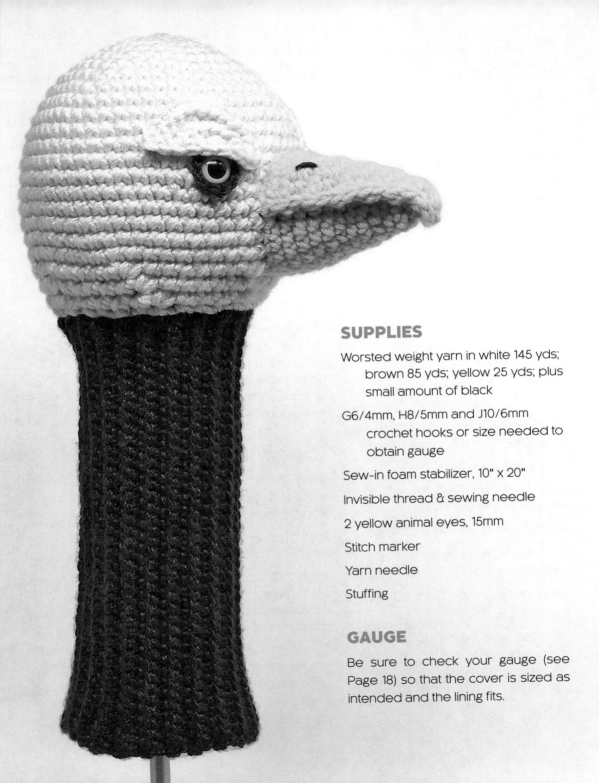

BALD EAGLE

SUPPLIES

Worsted weight yarn in white 145 yds; brown 85 yds; yellow 25 yds; plus small amount of black

G6/4mm, H8/5mm and J10/6mm crochet hooks or size needed to obtain gauge

Sew-in foam stabilizer, 10" x 20"

Invisible thread & sewing needle

2 yellow animal eyes, 15mm

Stitch marker

Yarn needle

Stuffing

GAUGE

Be sure to check your gauge (see Page 18) so that the cover is sized as intended and the lining fits.

HEAD COVER

With J10/6mm hook and 2 strands of white yarn held together, make a magic ring, ch 1.

Rnd 1: 6 sc in ring, pull ring closed tight (6 sts).

Rnd 2: 2 sc in each st around. Place marker for beginning of rnd and move marker up as each rnd is completed (12 sts).

Rnd 3: *sc in next st, 2 sc in next st* 6 times (18 sts).

Rnd 4: *sc in next 2 sts, 2 sc in next st* 6 times (24 sts).

Rnd 5: *sc in next 3 sts, 2 sc in next st* 6 times (30 sts).

Rnd 6: *sc in next 4 sts, 2 sc in next st* 6 times (36 sts).

Rnd 7: *sc in next 5 sts, 2 sc in next st* 6 times (42 sts).

Rnd 8: *sc in next 6 sts, 2 sc in next st* 6 times (48 sts).

Rnds 9-19: sc in each st around.

Rnd 20: *sc in next 6 sts, sc2tog* 6 times (42 sts).

Rnd 21: *sc in next 5 sts, sc2tog* 6 times (36 sts).

Rnd 22: *sc in next 4 sts, sc2tog* 6 times (30 sts).

Fasten off.

RIBBING

With H8/5mm crochet hook and a single strand of brown yarn, ch 41 loosely.

Note: A chain 1 at the beginning of a row is for turning your work and does not count as a stitch.

Work all rows in **back loops only** (see Page 13).

Row 1: sc in 2nd ch from hook and in each remaining ch across (40 sts).

Rows 2-42: ch 1, turn, sc in each st across (40 sts).

Do not fasten off. Pin last row and foundation ch row right sides together. Ch 1, sl st in each st across through both layers to form a tube. Fasten off.

LOWER BEAK

With H8/5mm crochet hook and a single strand of yellow yarn, make a magic ring, ch 1.

Rnd 1: 6 sc in ring, pull ring closed tight (6 sts).

Rnds 2-3: sc in each st around. Place marker for beginning of rnd and move marker up as each rnd is completed.

Tip: Push with a finger on the center of Rnd 1 to pop the round up to start shaping the cone.

Rnd 4: 2 sc in each st around (12 sts).

Rnds 5-6: sc in each st around.

Rnd 7: *sc in next st, 2 sc in next st* 6 times (18 sts).

Rnds 8-9: sc in each st around.

Rnd 10: *sc in next 2 sts, 2 sc in next st* 6 times (24 sts).

Rnds 11-12: sc in each st around.

Fasten off.

UPPER BEAK

To create this triangular shape, you will decrease one st in every row.

With H8/5mm crochet hook and a single strand of yellow yarn, ch 14.

Note: A chain 1 at the beginning of a row is for turning your work and does not count as a stitch.

Row 1: sc in 2nd ch from hook and in each remaining ch across (13 sts).

Rows 2-13: ch 1, turn, skip next st, sc in each remaining st across. You will end with 1 stitch on your hook. Sl st in each st around perimeter of triangle making 3 sts in same st at corners. Fasten off.

EYELID (MAKE 2)

With H8/5mm crochet hook and a single strand of white yarn, ch 2.

Note: A chain 1 at the beginning of a row is for turning your work and does not count as a stitch.

Work all rows in **back loops only** (see Page 13).

Row 1: 3 sc in 2nd ch from hook.

Row 2: ch 1, turn, 2 sc in next 3 sts (6 sts).

Row 3: ch 1, turn, *sc in next st, 2 sc in next st* 3 times (9 sts).

Row 4: ch 1, turn, *sc in next 2 sts, 2 sc in next st* 3 times (12 sts).

Row 5: ch 1, turn, *sc in next 3 sts, 2 sc in next st* 3 times (15 sts).

Row 6: ch 1, do not turn, continue across straight side making one sc in each st across. (Hold starting tail across straight side and crochet over tail as you work.) Sl st in next st. Fasten off.

EYE RIM (MAKE 2)

With G6/4mm crochet hook and a single strand of black yarn, make a magic ring, ch 1.

Rnd 1: 5 sc in ring, pull ring closed almost tight (5 sts).

Rnd 2: 2 sc in each st around (10 sts).

Sl st in next st. Fasten off.

ASSEMBLY

Stretch Ribbing open wide and insert Head Cover, right sides together, so that open edge of Head Cover meets an open end of Ribbing. Adjust so that center back of Head Cover meets seam of Ribbing. Pin in place, stretching Ribbing open and easing edge of Head Cover evenly around. Whip Stitch together with invisible thread. Weave in yarn ends.

With black yarn, embroider 2 straight sts on top of Upper Beak, about 1/2" long, for nostrils. Stuff Lower Beak. Sew beak sections together so that tip of Upper Beak curves down over tip of Lower Beak. Mark position of Beak on Head Cover with circle template (see Page 98). Sew Beak in place.

Insert stem of animal eyes through center of Eye Rims then into Head Cover and attach; or cut off stem, glue eye to Rim and sew in place (see Page 8). Sew Eyelids at a slight angle over Eyes, sloping downward toward Beak.

LINING

See Page 16 for how to make and attach the foam lining. This will provide structure for the Head Cover and more protection for the golf club. ♦

LADYBUG

SUPPLIES

Worsted weight yarn in red 145 yds; black 120 yds; plus small amount of white

H8/5mm and J10/6mm crochet hooks or size needed to obtain gauge

Sew-in foam stabilizer, 10" x 20"

Invisible thread & sewing needle

2 white animal eyes, 15mm

Stitch marker

Yarn needle

Stuffing

GAUGE

Be sure to check your gauge (see Page 18) so that the cover is sized as intended and the lining fits.

HEAD COVER

With J10/6mm hook and 2 strands of red yarn held together, make a magic ring, ch 1.

Rnd 1: 6 sc in ring, pull ring closed tight (6 sts).

Rnd 2: 2 sc in each st around. Place marker for beginning of rnd and move marker up as each rnd is completed (12 sts).

Rnd 3: *sc in next st, 2 sc in next st* 6 times (18 sts).

Rnd 4: *sc in next 2 sts, 2 sc in next st* 6 times (24 sts).

Rnd 5: *sc in next 3 sts, 2 sc in next st* 6 times (30 sts).

Rnd 6: *sc in next 4 sts, 2 sc in next st* 6 times (36 sts).

Rnd 7: *sc in next 5 sts, 2 sc in next st* 6 times (42 sts).

Rnd 8: *sc in next 6 sts, 2 sc in next st* 6 times (48 sts).

Rnds 9-19: sc in each st around.

Rnd 20: *sc in next 6 sts, sc2tog* 6 times (42 sts).

Rnd 21: *sc in next 5 sts, sc2tog* 6 times (36 sts).

Rnd 22: *sc in next 4 sts, sc2tog* 6 times (30 sts).

Fasten off.

RIBBING

With H8/5mm crochet hook and a single strand of black yarn, ch 41 loosely.

Note: A chain 1 at the beginning of a row is for turning your work and does not count as a stitch.

Work all rows in **back loops only** (see Page 13).

Row 1: sc in 2nd ch from hook and in each remaining ch across (40 sts).

Rows 2-42: ch 1, turn, sc in each st across (40 sts).

Do not fasten off. Pin last row and foundation ch row right sides together. Ch 1, sl st in each st across through both layers to form a tube. Fasten off.

HEAD

With H8/5mm hook and 2 strands of black yarn held together, make a magic ring, ch 1.

Rnd 1: 6 sc in ring, pull ring closed tight (6 sts).

Rnd 2: 2 sc in each st around. Place marker for beginning of rnd and move marker up as each rnd is completed (12 sts).

Rnd 3: *sc in next st, 2 sc in next st* 6 times (18 sts).

Rnd 4: *sc in next 2 sts, 2 sc in next st* 6 times (24 sts).

Rnds 5-7: sc in each st around.

Sl st in next st. Fasten off.

ANTENNA (MAKE 2)

With H8/5mm hook and 2 strands of black yarn held together, ch 10 tightly. Fasten off. Cut yarn close to knot at one end.

DOT (MAKE 11)

With H8/5mm hook and a single strand of black yarn, make a magic ring, ch 1.

Rnd 1: 6 sc in ring, pull ring closed tight (6 sts).

Rnd 2: 2 sc in each st around. Place marker for beginning of rnd and move marker up as each rnd is completed (12 sts).

Sl st in next st. Fasten off. Weave in ends.

ASSEMBLY

Stretch Ribbing open wide and insert Head Cover, right sides together, so that open edge of Head Cover meets an open end of Ribbing. Adjust so that center back of Head Cover meets seam of Ribbing. Pin in place, stretching

Ribbing open and easing edge of Head Cover evenly around. Whip Stitch together with invisible thread. Weave in yarn ends.

Attach animal eyes to Head (see Page 8). Pull long tails from Antennae through Head to wrong side and knot the tails together. If you would like to stiffen the antennae, run a needle and thread up and down through the center several times. With white yarn, embroider a V-shaped mouth. Mark position of Head on Head Cover with circle template (see Page 98). Stuff Head and sew in place. Sew on Dots.

LINING

See Page 16 for how to make and attach the foam lining. This will provide structure for the Head Cover and more protection for the golf club. ♦

DEER

SUPPLIES

Worsted weight yarn in tan 245 yds; white 30 yds; brown 30 yds

H8/5mm and J10/6mm crochet hooks or size needed to obtain gauge

Sew-in foam stabilizer, 10" x 20"

Invisible thread & sewing needle

2 black animal eyes, 15mm

Black triangle animal nose, 21mm

Stitch marker

Yarn needle

Stuffing

GAUGE

Be sure to check your gauge (see Page 18) so that the cover is sized as intended and the lining fits.

HEAD COVER

With J10/6mm hook and 2 strands of tan yarn held together, make a magic ring, ch 1.

Rnd 1: 6 sc in ring, pull ring closed tight (6 sts).

Rnd 2: 2 sc in each st around. Place marker for beginning of rnd and move marker up as each rnd is completed (12 sts).

Rnd 3: *sc in next st, 2 sc in next st* 6 times (18 sts).

Rnd 4: *sc in next 2 sts, 2 sc in next st* 6 times (24 sts).

Rnd 5: *sc in next 3 sts, 2 sc in next st* 6 times (30 sts).

Rnd 6: *sc in next 4 sts, 2 sc in next st* 6 times (36 sts).

Rnd 7: *sc in next 5 sts, 2 sc in next st* 6 times (42 sts).

Rnd 8: *sc in next 6 sts, 2 sc in next st* 6 times (48 sts).

Rnds 9-19: sc in each st around.

Rnd 20: *sc in next 6 sts, sc2tog* 6 times (42 sts).

Rnd 21: *sc in next 5 sts, sc2tog* 6 times (36 sts).

Rnd 22: *sc in next 4 sts, sc2tog* 6 times (30 sts).

Fasten off.

RIBBING

With H8/5mm crochet hook and a single strand of tan yarn, ch 41 loosely.

Note: A chain 1 at the beginning of a row is for turning your work and does not count as a stitch.

Work all rows in **back loops only** (see Page 13).

Row 1: sc in 2nd ch from hook and in each remaining ch across (40 sts).

Rows 2-16: ch 1, turn, sc in each st across; change to white yarn in last st (40 sts).

Row 17: ch 1, turn, sc in next 8 sts, change to tan yarn, sc in next 32 sts (40 sts).

Row 18: ch 1, turn, sc in next 31 sts, change to white yarn, sc in next 9 sts (40 sts).

Row 19: ch 1, turn, sc in next 10 sts, change to tan yarn, sc in next 30 sts (40 sts).

Row 20: ch 1, turn, sc in next 29 sts, change to white yarn, sc in next 11 sts (40 sts).

Row 21: ch 1, turn, sc in next 11 sts, change to tan yarn, sc in next 29 sts (40 sts).

Row 22: ch 1, turn, sc in next 30 sts, change to white yarn, sc in next 10 sts (40 sts).

Row 23: ch 1, turn, sc in next 9 sts, change to tan yarn, sc in next 31 sts (40 sts).

Row 24: ch 1, turn, sc in next 32 sts, change to white yarn, sc in next 8 sts; change to tan yarn in last st (40 sts).

Rows 25-42: ch 1, turn, sc in each st across (40 sts).

Do not fasten off. Pin last row and foundation ch row right sides together. Ch 1, sl st in each st across through both layers to form a tube. Fasten off.

SNOUT

With J10/6mm hook and 2 strands of white yarn held together, make a magic ring, ch 1.

Rnd 1: 6 sc in ring, pull ring closed almost tight (6 sts).

Rnd 2: *sc in next st, 2 sc in next st* 3 times. Place marker for beginning of rnd and move marker up as each rnd is completed (9 sts).

Rnd 3: *sc in next 2 sts, 2 sc in next st* 3 times (12 sts).

Rnd 4: *sc in next 3 sts, 2 sc in next st* 3 times; change to tan yarn in last st (15 sts).

Rnd 5: *sc in next 4 sts, 2 sc in next st* 3 times (18 sts).

Rnd 6: *sc in next 5 sts, 2 sc in next st* 3 times (21 sts).

Rnd 7: *sc in next 6 sts, 2 sc in next st* 3 times (24 sts).

Rnds 8-10: sc in each st around.

Fasten off.

EYE RIM (MAKE 2)

With H8/5mm hook and a single strand of white yarn, make a magic ring, ch 1.

Rnd 1: 8 sc in ring, pull ring closed almost tight (8 sts).

Rnd 2a: 2 sc in next 3 sts (6 sts).

Point: ch 2 and sc in 2nd ch from hook, sc in next st.

Rnd 2b: 2 sc in next 3 sts (6 sts).

Point: ch 2 and sc in 2nd ch from hook, sc in next st.

Sl st in next st. Fasten off.

OUTER EAR (MAKE 2)

With J10/6mm hook and 2 strands of tan yarn held together, make a magic ring, ch 1.

Rnd 1: 6 sc in ring, pull ring closed tight (6 sts).

Rnd 2: 2 sc in each st around. Place marker for beginning of rnd and move marker up as each rnd is completed. (12 sts).

Rnd 3: *sc in next st, 2 sc in next st* 6 times (18 sts).

Rnds 4-6: sc in each st around. Fasten off.

INNER EAR (MAKE 2)

With H8/5mm hook and a single strand of white yarn, ch 1.

Rnd 1: 6 sc in ring, pull ring closed tight (6 sts).

Rnd 2: 2 sc in each st around. Place marker for beginning of rnd and move marker up as each rnd is completed. (12 sts).

Rnd 3: *sc in next st, 2 sc in next st* 6 times (18 sts).

Rnd 4: *sc in next 2 sts, 2 sc in next st* 6 times (24 sts).

Rnd 5: sc in each st around. Fasten off.

ANTLER (MAKE 2)

Be sure to work in good light. The Antler is made in 2 parts.

Part A

With J10/6mm hook and 2 strands of brown yarn held together, make a magic ring, ch 1.

Rnd 1: 6 sc in ring, pull ring closed tight (6 sts).

Rnds 2-?: sc in each st around until piece is 3 1/2" long.

Fasten off.

Part B

Follow instructions for Part A to make a piece that is 1 1/2" long.

ASSEMBLY

Stretch Ribbing open wide and insert Head Cover, right sides together, so that open edge of Head Cover meets edge of Ribbing that has the white patch. Adjust so that center back of Head Cover meets seam of Ribbing. Pin in place, stretching Ribbing open and easing edge of Head Cover evenly around. Whip Stitch together with invisible thread. Weave in yarn ends.

Attach nose to tip of Snout. Mark position of Snout on Head Cover with circle template (see Page 98). Stuff Snout and sew in place.

Insert stem of animal eyes through center of Eye Rims then into Head Cover and attach. Sew edge of Eye Rims to Head Cover with invisible thread. (Or cut off stem, glue eye to Rim and sew in place, see Page 8).

Put Inner Ear inside Outer Ear. Sew Inner Ear in place with invisible thread. Pull on tail of Outer Ear to make a teardrop shape and make a few stitches at tip to hold the shape. Sew Ear to Head Cover.

Sew Parts A and B of Antlers together. Sew Antlers to Head Cover with invisible thread.

Note: See Title Page for a side view photo of Deer.

LINING

See Page 16 for how to make and attach the foam lining. This will provide structure for the Head Cover and more protection for the golf club. ♦

MALLARD

SUPPLIES

Worsted weight yarn in dark green 145 yds; brown 65 yds; white 20 yds; plus small amount of yellow and black

H8/5mm and J10/6mm crochet hooks or size needed to obtain gauge

Sew-in foam stabilizer, 10" x 20"

Invisible thread & sewing needle

2 copper or yellow animal eyes, 18mm

Stitch marker

Yarn needle

Stuffing

GAUGE

Be sure to check your gauge (see Page 18) so that the cover is sized as intended and the lining fits.

HEAD COVER

With J10/6mm hook and 2 strands of dark green yarn held together, make a magic ring, ch 1.

Rnd 1: 6 sc in ring, pull ring closed tight (6 sts).

Rnd 2: 2 sc in each st around. Place marker for beginning of rnd and move marker up as each rnd is completed (12 sts).

Rnd 3: *sc in next st, 2 sc in next st* 6 times (18 sts).

Rnd 4: *sc in next 2 sts, 2 sc in next st* 6 times (24 sts).

Rnd 5: *sc in next 3 sts, 2 sc in next st* 6 times (30 sts).

Rnd 6: *sc in next 4 sts, 2 sc in next st* 6 times (36 sts).

Rnd 7: *sc in next 5 sts, 2 sc in next st* 6 times (42 sts).

Rnd 8: *sc in next 6 sts, 2 sc in next st* 6 times (48 sts).

Rnds 9-19: sc in each st around.

Rnd 20: *sc in next 6 sts, sc2tog* 6 times (42 sts).

Rnd 21: *sc in next 5 sts, sc2tog* 6 times (36 sts).

Rnd 22: *sc in next 4 sts, sc2tog* 6 times (30 sts).

Fasten off.

RIBBING

A white stripe that is 5 stitches deep creates the Mallard's neck band.

With H8/5mm crochet hook and a single strand of brown yarn, ch 41 loosely.

Note: A chain 1 at the beginning of a row is for turning your work and does not count as a stitch.

Work all rows in **back loops only** (see Page 13).

Row 1: sc in 2nd ch from hook and in each remaining ch across; change to white after 35 sts (40 sts).

Row 2: ch 1, turn, sc in each st across; change to brown after 5 sts (40 sts).

Row 3: ch 1, turn, sc in each st across; change to white after 35 sts (40 sts).

Rows 4-42: continue alternating Rows 2 and 3.

Do not fasten off. Pin last row and foundation ch row right sides together. Ch 1, sl st in each st across through both layers to form a tube. Fasten off.

BEAK

With H8/5mm crochet hook and a single strand of yellow yarn, ch 6 loosely.

Rnd 1: sc in 2nd ch from hook, sc in next 3 chs, 3 sc in next ch, working on opposite side of foundation ch, sc in next 3 chs, 2 sc in next ch (12 sts).

Rnds 2-4: sc in each st around. Place marker for beginning of rnd and move marker up as each rnd is completed.

Rnd 5: *2 sc in next st, sc in next 5 sts* 2 times (14 sts).

Rnd 6: sc in each st around.

Rnd 7: *2 sc in next st, sc in next 6 sts* 2 times (16 sts).

Rnd 8: sc in each st around.

Rnd 9: *2 sc in next st, sc in next 7 sts* 2 times (18 sts).

Rnd 10: sc in each st around.

Fasten off.

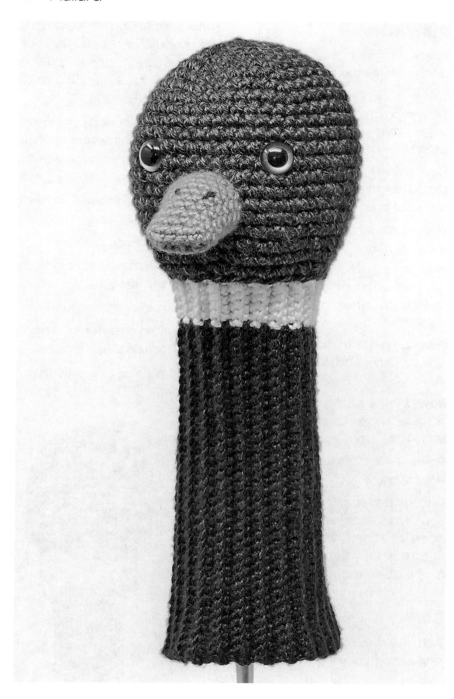

ASSEMBLY

Stretch Ribbing open wide and insert Head Cover, right sides together, so that open edge of Head Cover meets white end of Ribbing. Adjust so that center back of Head Cover meets seam of Ribbing. Pin in place, stretching Ribbing open and easing edge of Head Cover evenly around. Whip Stitch together with invisible thread. Weave in yarn ends.

With a single strand of black yarn, embroider 2 stitches on top of Beak for nostrils. Mark position of Beak on Head Cover with oval template (see Page 98). Stuff Beak and sew in place with invisible thread.

Attach eyes (see Page 8).

LINING

See Page 16 for how to make and attach the foam lining. This will provide structure for the Head Cover and more protection for the golf club. ♦

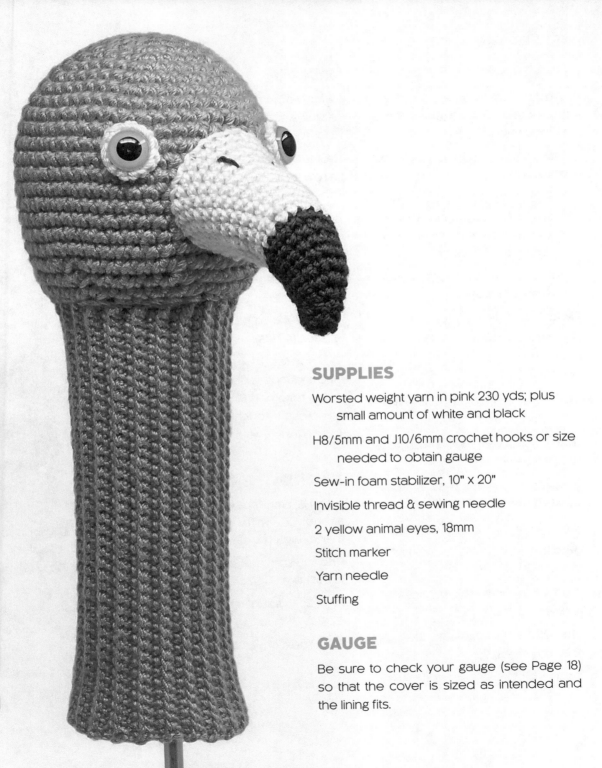

FLAMINGO

SUPPLIES

Worsted weight yarn in pink 230 yds; plus
    small amount of white and black

H8/5mm and J10/6mm crochet hooks or size
    needed to obtain gauge

Sew-in foam stabilizer, 10" x 20"

Invisible thread & sewing needle

2 yellow animal eyes, 18mm

Stitch marker

Yarn needle

Stuffing

GAUGE

Be sure to check your gauge (see Page 18)
so that the cover is sized as intended and
the lining fits.

HEAD COVER

With J10/6mm hook and 2 strands of pink yarn held together, make a magic ring, ch 1.

Rnd 1: 6 sc in ring, pull ring closed tight (6 sts).

Rnd 2: 2 sc in each st around. Place marker for beginning of rnd and move marker up as each rnd is completed (12 sts).

Rnd 3: *sc in next st, 2 sc in next st* 6 times (18 sts).

Rnd 4: *sc in next 2 sts, 2 sc in next st* 6 times (24 sts).

Rnd 5: *sc in next 3 sts, 2 sc in next st* 6 times (30 sts).

Rnd 6: *sc in next 4 sts, 2 sc in next st* 6 times (36 sts).

Rnd 7: *sc in next 5 sts, 2 sc in next st* 6 times (42 sts).

Rnd 8: *sc in next 6 sts, 2 sc in next st* 6 times (48 sts).

Rnds 9-19: sc in each st around.

Rnd 20: *sc in next 6 sts, sc2tog* 6 times (42 sts).

Rnd 21: *sc in next 5 sts, sc2tog* 6 times (36 sts).

Rnd 22: *sc in next 4 sts, sc2tog* 6 times (30 sts).

Fasten off.

RIBBING

With H8/5mm crochet hook and a single strand of pink yarn, ch 41 loosely.

Note: A chain 1 at the beginning of a row is for turning your work and does not count as a stitch.

Work all rows in **back loops only** (see Page 13).

Row 1: sc in 2nd ch from hook and in each remaining ch across (40 sts).

Rows 2-42: ch 1, turn, sc in each st across (40 sts).

Do not fasten off. Pin last row and foundation ch row right sides together. Ch 1, sl st in each st across through both layers to form a tube. Fasten off.

EYE RIM (MAKE 2)

With H8/5mm hook and a single strand of white yarn, make a magic ring, ch 1.

Rnd 1: 6 sc in ring, pull ring closed almost tight (6 sts).

Rnd 2: 2 sc in each st around (12 sts).

Sl st in next st. Fasten off.

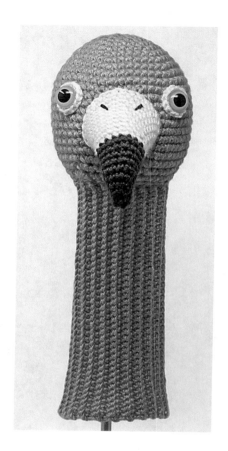

BEAK

With H8/5mm hook and a single strand of black yarn, make a magic ring, ch 1.

Rnd 1: 5 sc in ring, pull ring closed tight (5 sts).

Rnd 2: sc in next 4 sts, 2 sc in next st (6 sts).

Rnd 3: sc in next 5 sts, 2 sc in next st (7 sts).

Rnd 4: sc in next 6 sts, 2 sc in next st (8 sts).

Rnd 5: *sc in next 3 sts, 2 sc in next st* 2 times (10 sts).

Rnd 6: *sc in next 4 sts, 2 sc in next st* 2 times (12 sts).

Rnd 7: sc in each st around.

Rnd 8: *sc in next 5 sts, 2 sc in next st* 2 times (14 sts).

Rnd 9: sc in each st around.

Rnd 10: *sc in next 6 sts, 2 sc in next st* 2 times (16 sts).

Rnd 11: sc in each st around; change to white yarn in last st.

Rnd 12: *sc in next 7 sts, 2 sc in next st* 2 times (18 sts).

Rnd 13: sc in each st around.

Rnd 14: *sc in next 8 sts, 2 sc in next st* 2 times (20 sts).

Rnd 15: sc in each st around.

Rnd 16: *sc in next 9 sts, 2 sc in next st* 2 times (22 sts).

Rnd 17: sc in each st around.

Rnd 18: *sc in next 10 sts, 2 sc in next st* 2 times (24 sts).

Rnd 19: sc in each st around.

Rnd 20: *sc in next 11 sts, 2 sc in next st* 2 times (26 sts).

Rnd 21-22: sc in each st around.

Rnd 23: *sc in next 12 sts, 2 sc in next st* 2 times (28 sts).

Fasten off with long tail. Stuff with fiberfill. With yarn needle, run long tail through stitches from base of tail to tip of Beak, passing through the actual stitches, not through the stuffing (see Figure A). Pull long tail like a drawstring to shape Beak into a curve, knot to hold shape, and run needle back through Beak to opening edge.

Note: A small v-shaped notch in edge of Beak may appear at base of drawstring. If so, close it up with a stitch or two.

ASSEMBLY

Stretch Ribbing open wide and insert Head Cover, right sides together, so that open edge of Head Cover meets an open end of Ribbing. Adjust so that center back of Head Cover meets seam of Ribbing. Pin in place, stretching Ribbing open and easing edge of Head Cover evenly around. Whip Stitch together with invisible thread. Weave in yarn ends.

Mark position of Beak on Head Cover with circle template (see Page 98). Sew Beak in place. Embroider 2 straight stitches on Beak with black yarn for nostrils.

Insert stem of animal eyes through center of Eye Rims then into Head Cover and attach; or cut off stem, glue eye to Rim and sew in place (see Page 8).

LINING

See Page 16 for how to make and attach the foam lining. This will provide structure for the Head Cover and more protection for the golf club. ◆

FIGURE A

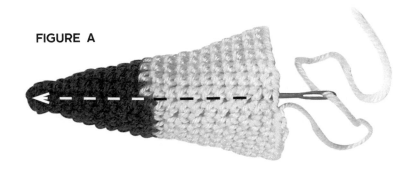

LABRADOR RETRIEVER

SUPPLIES

Worsted weight yarn in tan 300 yds; purple 20 yds; plus small amount of gray and black

H8/5mm and J10/6mm crochet hooks or size needed to obtain gauge

Sew-in foam stabilizer, 10" x 20"

Invisible thread & sewing needle

2 black animal eyes, 18mm

Black triangle animal nose, 21mm

Stitch marker

Yarn needle

Stuffing

GAUGE

Be sure to check your gauge (see Page 18) so that the cover is sized as intended and the lining fits.

HEAD COVER

With J10/6mm hook and 2 strands of tan yarn held together, make a magic ring, ch 1.

Rnd 1: 6 sc in ring, pull ring closed tight (6 sts).

Rnd 2: 2 sc in each st around. Place marker for beginning of rnd and move marker up as each rnd is completed (12 sts).

Rnd 3: *sc in next st, 2 sc in next st* 6 times (18 sts).

Rnd 4: *sc in next 2 sts, 2 sc in next st* 6 times (24 sts).

Rnd 5: *sc in next 3 sts, 2 sc in next st* 6 times (30 sts).

Rnd 6: *sc in next 4 sts, 2 sc in next st* 6 times (36 sts).

Rnd 7: *sc in next 5 sts, 2 sc in next st* 6 times (42 sts).

Rnd 8: *sc in next 6 sts, 2 sc in next st* 6 times (48 sts).

Rnds 9-19: sc in each st around.

Rnd 20: *sc in next 6 sts, sc2tog* 6 times (42 sts).

Rnd 21: *sc in next 5 sts, sc2tog* 6 times (36 sts).

Rnd 22: *sc in next 4 sts, sc2tog* 6 times (30 sts).

Fasten off.

TAG

With J10/6mm hook and 2 strands of gray yarn held together, make a magic ring, ch 1.

Rnd 1: 6 sc in ring, pull ring closed tight (6 sts).

Rnd 2: 2 sc in each st around (12 sts). Sl st in next st. For Tag's loop, ch 10. Fasten off.

RIBBING

A purple stripe that is 5 stitches deep creates the Dog's collar.

With H8/5mm crochet hook and a single strand of tan yarn, ch 41 loosely.

Note: A chain 1 at the beginning of a row is for turning your work and does not count as a stitch.

Work all rows in **back loops only** (see Page 13).

Row 1: sc in 2nd ch from hook and in each remaining ch across; change to purple after 35 sts (40 sts).

Row 2: ch 1, turn, sc in each st across; change to tan after 5 sts (40 sts).

Row 3: ch 1, turn, sc in each st across; change to purple after 35 sts (40 sts).

Rows 4-42: continue alternating Rows 2 and 3.

Do not fasten off. Pin last row and foundation ch row right sides together. Ch 1, sl st in each st across through both layers to form a tube. Fasten off. This seam is center back of Ribbing.

Thread needle with tail of Tag. Hold Tag in position at center front of Ribbing. Wrap ch sts around purple stripe and push needle from back to front at base of purple stripe. Sew first and last sts of ch together.

EAR (MAKE 2)

With J10/6mm hook and 2 strands of tan yarn held together, ch 5 loosely.

Note: A chain 1 at the beginning of a row is for turning your work and does not count as a stitch.

Row 1: sc in 2nd ch from hook and in each remaining ch across (4 sts). This is top of Ear.

Row 2: ch 1, turn, sc in each st across.

Row 3: ch 1, turn, 2 sc in next st, sc in next 2 sts, 2 sc in next st (6 sts).

Rows 4-5: ch 1, turn, sc in each st across.

Row 6: ch 1, turn, 2 sc in next st, sc in next 4 sts, 2 sc in next st (8 sts).

Rows 7-17: ch 1, turn, sc in each st across.

Row 18: ch 1, turn, sc2tog, sc in next 4 sts, sc2tog (6 sts).

Row 19: ch 1, turn, sc in each st across.

Rnd 20: ch 1, do not turn, sc around next 3 sides working a sc in end of each row and in each st across top. Join with sl st to 1st st. Fasten off.

SNOUT

With J10/6mm hook and 2 strands of tan yarn held together, make a magic ring, ch 1.

Rnd 1: 6 sc in ring, pull ring closed almost tight (6 sts).

Rnd 2: 2 sc in each st around. Place marker for beginning of rnd and move marker up as each rnd is completed (12 sts).

Rnd 3: *sc in next st, 2 sc in next st* 6 times (18 sts).

Rnd 4: *sc in next 2 sts, 2 sc in next st* 6 times (24 sts).

Rnds 5-7: sc in each st around.

Fasten off.

ASSEMBLY

Stretch Ribbing open wide and insert Head Cover, right sides together, so that open edge of Head Cover meets purple end of Ribbing. Adjust so that center back of Head Cover meets seam of Ribbing. Pin in place, stretching Ribbing open and easing edge of Head Cover evenly around. Whip Stitch together with invisible thread. Weave in yarn ends.

With black yarn, embroider a vertical stitch from center of Snout to groove between Rnds 4-5. Attach nose to center of Snout. Mark position of Snout on Head Cover with circle template (see Page 98). Stuff Snout and sew in place with invisible thread.

Attach eyes (see Page 8).

To get "lift" at top of Ears, hold Ear in position, then flip like you are turning the page of a book so that right side of Ear faces right side of Head Cover. Whip stitch in place, then flip Ear down.

LINING

See Page 16 for how to make and attach the foam lining. This will provide structure for the Head Cover and more protection for the golf club. ♦

PENGUIN

SUPPLIES

Worsted weight yarn in black 215 yds; white 40 yds; plus small amount of orange

H8/5mm and J10/6mm crochet hooks or size needed to obtain gauge

Sew-in foam stabilizer, 10" x 20"

Invisible thread & sewing needle

2 blue animal eyes, 20mm

Stitch marker

Yarn needle

Stuffing

GAUGE

Be sure to check your gauge (see Page 18) so that the cover is sized as intended and the lining fits.

HEAD COVER

With J10/6mm hook and 2 strands of black yarn held together, make a magic ring, ch 1.

Rnd 1: 6 sc in ring, pull ring closed tight (6 sts).

Rnd 2: 2 sc in each st around. Place marker for beginning of rnd and move marker up as each rnd is completed (12 sts).

Rnd 3: *sc in next st, 2 sc in next st* 6 times (18 sts).

Rnd 4: *sc in next 2 sts, 2 sc in next st* 6 times (24 sts).

Rnd 5: *sc in next 3 sts, 2 sc in next st* 6 times (30 sts).

Rnd 6: *sc in next 4 sts, 2 sc in next st* 6 times (36 sts).

Rnd 7: *sc in next 5 sts, 2 sc in next st* 6 times (42 sts).

Rnd 8: *sc in next 6 sts, 2 sc in next st* 6 times (48 sts).

Rnds 9-19: sc in each st around.

Rnd 20: *sc in next 6 sts, sc2tog* 6 times (42 sts).

Rnd 21: *sc in next 5 sts, sc2tog* 6 times (36 sts).

Rnd 22: *sc in next 4 sts, sc2tog* 6 times (30 sts).

Fasten off.

RIBBING

With H8/5mm crochet hook and a single strand of black yarn, ch 41 loosely.

Note: A chain 1 at the beginning of a row is for turning your work and does not count as a stitch.

Work all rows in **back loops only** (see Page 13).

Row 1: sc in 2nd ch from hook and in each remaining ch across (40 sts).

Rows 2-17: ch 1, turn, sc in each st across; change to white yarn in last st (40 sts).

Rows 18-25: ch 1, turn, sc in each st across; change to black yarn in last st (40 sts).

Rows 26-42: ch 1, turn, sc in each st across (40 sts).

Do not fasten off. Pin last row and foundation ch row right sides together. Ch 1, sl st in each st across through both layers to form a tube. Fasten off.

UPPER FACE (MAKE 2)

With H8/5mm hook and a single strand of white yarn, ch 2.

Note: A chain 1 at the beginning of a row is for turning your work and does not count as a stitch.

Row 1: 3 sc in 2nd ch from hook.

Row 2: ch 1, turn, 2 sc in next 3 sts (6 sts).

Row 3: ch 1, turn, *sc in next st, 2 sc in next st* 3 times (9 sts).

Row 4: ch 1, turn, *sc in next 2 sts, 2 sc in next st* 3 times (12 sts).

Fasten off.

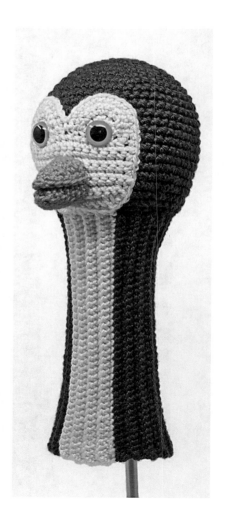

LOWER FACE

With H8/5mm hook and a single strand of white yarn, ch 17 loosely.

Note: A chain 1 at the beginning of a row is for turning your work and does not count as a stitch.

Row 1: sc in 2nd ch from hook and in each remaining ch across (16 sts).

Rows 2-7: ch 1, turn, sc in each st across (16 sts).

Row 8: ch 1, turn, sc2tog, sc in next 12 sts, sc2tog (14 sts).

Rows 9: ch 1, turn, sc2tog, sc in next 10 sts, sc2tog (12 sts).

Row 10: ch 1, turn, sc2tog, sc in next 8 sts, sc2tog (10 sts).

Fasten off. Sew Upper Face pieces to Lower Face. Fasten on at lower edge and sc around entire perimeter. Note: When you get to the top "V" (indentation at top of face), sl st instead of sc. Fasten off.

LOWER BEAK

With H8/5mm hook and a single strand of orange yarn, make a magic ring, ch 1.

Rnd 1: 6 sc in ring, pull ring closed tight (6 sts).

Rnd 2: *sc in next st, 2 sc in next st* 3 times (9 sts).

Tip: Push with a finger on the center of Rnd 1 to pop the round up to start shaping the cone.

Rnd 3: sc in each st around.

Rnd 4: *sc in next 2 sts, 2 sc in next st* 3 times (12 sts).

Rnd 5: sc in each st around.

Rnd 6: *sc in next 3 sts, 2 sc in next st* 3 times (15 sts).

Rnd 7: sc in each st around.

Rnd 8: *sc in next 4 sts, 2 sc in next st* 3 times (18 sts).

Sl st in next st. Fasten off.

UPPER BEAK

To create this triangular shape, you will decrease one st in every row.

With H8/5mm crochet hook and a single strand of orange yarn, ch 8.

Note: A chain 1 at the beginning of a row is for turning your work and does not count as a stitch.

Row 1: sc in 2nd ch from hook and in each remaining ch across (7 sts).

Row 2: ch 1, turn, skip next st, sc in each remaining st across (6 sts).

Row 3: ch 1, turn, skip next st, sc in each remaining st across (5 sts).

Row 4: ch 1, turn, skip next st, sc in each remaining st across (4 sts).

Row 5: ch 1, turn, skip next st, sc in each remaining st across (3 sts).

Row 6: ch 1, turn, skip next st, sc in each remaining st across (2 sts).

Rnd 7: do not turn, continue working forward and sc in each st around perimeter of piece making 3 sts in same st at back corners. Sl st in next st. Fasten off. Weave in ends.

ASSEMBLY

Stretch Ribbing open wide and insert Head Cover, right sides together, so that open edge of Head Cover meets an open end of Ribbing. Adjust so that center back of Head Cover meets seam of Ribbing. Pin in place, stretching Ribbing open and easing edge of Head Cover evenly around. Whip Stitch together with invisible thread. Weave in yarn ends.

Attach animal eyes to Face (see Page 8). Sew Face to Head Cover.

Sew Upper Beak to Lower Beak along back edge. Mark position of Beak on Head Cover with circle template (see Page 98). Stuff Beak and sew in place with invisible thread.

LINING

See Page 16 for how to make and attach the foam lining. This will provide structure for the Head Cover and more protection for the golf club. ♦

TABBY CAT

SUPPLIES

Worsted weight yarn in medium gray 120 yds; light gray 120 yds; plus small amount of pink and white

H8/5mm and J10/6mm crochet hooks or size needed to obtain gauge

Sew-in foam stabilizer, 10" x 20"

Invisible thread & sewing needle

2 green cat eyes, 21mm

Stitch marker

Yarn needle

GAUGE

Be sure to check your gauge (see Page 18) so that the cover is sized as intended and the lining fits.

HEAD COVER

The Head Cover is made by alternating 2 rnds of medium gray with 2 rnds of light gray. **Change to alternate color in last st of every other rnd.**

With J10/6mm hook and 2 strands of medium gray yarn held together, make a magic ring, ch 1.

Rnd 1: 6 sc in ring, pull ring closed tight (6 sts).

Rnd 2: 2 sc in each st around. Place marker for beginning of rnd and move marker up as each rnd is completed (12 sts).

Rnd 3: *sc in next st, 2 sc in next st* 6 times (18 sts).

Rnd 4: *sc in next 2 sts, 2 sc in next st* 6 times (24 sts).

Rnd 5: *sc in next 3 sts, 2 sc in next st* 6 times (30 sts).

Rnd 6: *sc in next 4 sts, 2 sc in next st* 6 times (36 sts).

Rnd 7: *sc in next 5 sts, 2 sc in next st* 6 times (42 sts).

Rnd 8: *sc in next 6 sts, 2 sc in next st* 6 times (48 sts).

Rnds 9-19: sc in each st around.

Rnd 20: *sc in next 6 sts, sc2tog* 6 times (42 sts).

Rnd 21: *sc in next 5 sts, sc2tog* 6 times (36 sts).

Rnd 22: *sc in next 4 sts, sc2tog* 6 times (30 sts).

Fasten off.

RIBBING

The Ribbing is made by alternating 2 rows of medium gray with 2 rows of light gray. **Change to alternate color in last st of every other row.**

With H8/5mm crochet hook and a single strand of medium gray yarn, ch 41 loosely.

Note: A chain 1 at the beginning of a row is for turning your work and does not count as a stitch.

Work all rows in **back loops only** (see Page 13).

Row 1: sc in 2nd ch from hook and in each remaining ch across (40 sts).

Rows 2-42: ch 1, turn, sc in each st across (40 sts).

Do not fasten off. Pin last row and foundation ch row right sides together. Ch 1, sl st in each st across through both layers to form a tube. Fasten off.

NOSE

H8/5mm crochet hook and a single strand of medium gray yarn, ch 7 loosely.

Note: A chain 1 at the beginning of a row is for turning your work and does not count as a stitch.

Row 1: sc in 2nd ch from hook and in each remaining ch across (6 sts).

Rows 2-9: ch 1, turn, sc in each st across; change to pink yarn in last st (6 sts).

Row 10: ch 1, turn, sc2tog, sc in next 2 sts, sc2tog (4 sts).

Row 11 ch 1, turn, sc2tog twice (2 sts).

Row 12: ch 1, turn, sc2tog (1 st).

Fasten off. Weave in ends except for pink ending tail.

MUZZLE

With H8/5mm crochet hook and a single strand of white yarn, make a magic ring, ch 1.

Rnd 1: 6 sc in ring, pull ring closed tight (6 sts).

Rnd 2: 2 sc in each st around. Place marker for beginning of rnd and move marker up as each rnd is completed (12 sts).

Rnds 3-9: sc in each st around.

Rnd 10: sc2tog 6 times (6 sts).

Fasten off and thread tail onto yarn needle. Weave needle down through center of each stitch around opening. Pull tail tight to close hole. Weave in end.

EAR (MAKE 2)

With hook size H8/5mm and a single strand of medium gray yarn, chain 2 loosely.

Note: A chain 1 at the beginning of a row is for turning your work and does not count as a stitch.

Row 1: 3 sc in 2nd chain from hook (3 sts).

Row 2: ch 1, turn, 2 sc in next st, sc in next 2 sts (4 sts).

Row 3: ch 1, turn, 2 sc in next st, sc in next 3 sts (5 sts).

Row 4: ch 1, turn, 2 sc in next st, sc in next 4 sts (6 sts).

Row 5: ch 1, turn, 2 sc in next st, sc in next 5 sts (7 sts).

Row 6: ch 1, turn, 2 sc in next st, sc in next 6 sts (8 sts).

Row 7: ch 1, turn, 2 sc in next st, sc in next 7 sts (9 sts).

Fasten off. Trim tails to 1 1/2". Repeat with pink yarn.

Place gray piece against pink piece, wrong sides together, tucking yarn tails between layers.

Hold work pink-side up. Using medium gray yarn, fasten on with single crochet (see Page 15) at

lower right corner. Single crochet around next 2 sides working each st through both ear pieces and making 3 sts in same st at top. (Refer to photos for Tiger Ears on Page 32.). Fasten off.

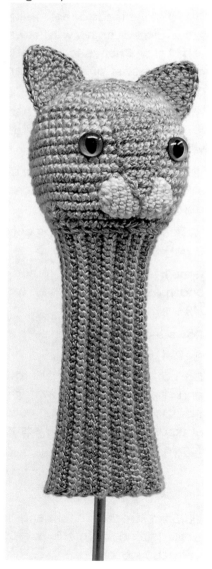

ASSEMBLY

Stretch Ribbing open wide and insert Head Cover, right sides together, so that open edge of Head Cover meets an open end of Ribbing. Adjust so that center back of Head Cover meets seam of Ribbing. Pin in place, stretching Ribbing open and easing edge of Head Cover evenly around. Whip Stitch together with invisible thread. Weave in yarn ends.

Thread yarn needle with pink tail of Nose. Position tip of Nose at center of Muzzle and pin in place. Wrap pink tail around lower half of Muzzle and push needle up from wrong side into pink area of Nose, pulling tight. Sew up and down thru pink tip of Nose and Muzzle to fasten them together. Sew Nose/Muzzle assembly to Head Cover with invisible thread. Attach eyes (see Page 8).

Sew layers of Ear together along open edge with invisible thread. Sew Ears slightly cupped to Head Cover.

LINING

See Page 16 for how to make and attach the foam lining. This will provide structure for the Head Cover and more protection for the golf club. ♦

BEAR

SUPPLIES

Worsted weight yarn in brown 260 yds
    and tan 35 yds

H8/5mm and J10/6mm crochet hooks
    or size needed to obtain gauge

Sew-in foam stabilizer, 10" x 20"

Invisible thread & sewing needle

2 brown animal eyes, 18mm

Black animal bear nose, 20mm

Stitch marker

Yarn needle

Stuffing

GAUGE

Be sure to check your gauge (see
Page 18) so that the cover is sized as
intended and the lining fits.

HEAD COVER

With J10/6mm hook and 2 strands of brown yarn held together, make a magic ring, ch 1.

Rnd 1: 6 sc in ring, pull ring closed tight (6 sts).

Rnd 2: 2 sc in each st around. Place marker for beginning of rnd and move marker up as each rnd is completed (12 sts).

Rnd 3: *sc in next st, 2 sc in next st* 6 times (18 sts).

Rnd 4: *sc in next 2 sts, 2 sc in next st* 6 times (24 sts).

Rnd 5: *sc in next 3 sts, 2 sc in next st* 6 times (30 sts).

Rnd 6: *sc in next 4 sts, 2 sc in next st* 6 times (36 sts).

Rnd 7: *sc in next 5 sts, 2 sc in next st* 6 times (42 sts).

Rnd 8: *sc in next 6 sts, 2 sc in next st* 6 times (48 sts).

Rnds 9-19: sc in each st around.

Rnd 20: *sc in next 6 sts, sc2tog* 6 times (42 sts).

Rnd 21: *sc in next 5 sts, sc2tog* 6 times (36 sts).

Rnd 22: *sc in next 4 sts, sc2tog* 6 times (30 sts).

Fasten off.

RIBBING

With H8/5mm crochet hook and a single strand of brown yarn, ch 41 loosely.

Note: A chain 1 at the beginning of a row is for turning your work and does not count as a stitch.

Work all rows in **back loops only** (see Page 13).

Row 1: sc in 2nd ch from hook and in each remaining ch across (40 sts).

Rows 2-16: ch 1, turn, sc in each st across; change to tan yarn in last st (40 sts).

Row 17: ch 1, turn, sc in next 8 sts, change to brown yarn, sc in next 32 sts (40 sts).

Row 18: ch 1, turn, sc in next 31 sts, change to tan yarn, sc in next 9 sts (40 sts).

Row 19: ch 1, turn, sc in next 10 sts, change to brown yarn, sc in next 30 sts (40 sts).

Row 20: ch 1, turn, sc in next 29 sts, change to tan yarn, sc in next 11 sts (40 sts).

Row 21: ch 1, turn, sc in next 11 sts, change to brown yarn, sc in next 29 sts (40 sts).

Row 22: ch 1, turn, sc in next 30 sts, change to tan yarn, sc in next 10 sts (40 sts).

Row 23: ch 1, turn, sc in next 9 sts, change to brown yarn, sc in next 31 sts (40 sts).

Row 24: ch 1, turn, sc in next 32 sts, change to tan yarn, sc in next 8 sts; change to brown yarn in last st (40 sts).

Rows 25-42: ch 1, turn, sc in each st across (40 sts).

Do not fasten off. Pin last row and foundation ch row right sides together. Ch 1, sl st in each st across through both layers to form a tube. Fasten off.

SNOUT

With J10/6mm hook and 2 strands of tan yarn held together, make a magic ring, ch 1.

Rnd 1: 6 sc in ring, pull ring closed almost tight (6 sts).

Rnd 2: 2 sc in each st around. Place marker for beginning of rnd and move marker up as each rnd is completed (12 sts).

Rnd 3: sc in each st around.

Rnd 4: *sc in next st, 2 sc in next st* 6 times (18 sts).

Rnd 5: sc in each st around.

Rnd 6: *sc in next 2 sts, 2 sc in next st* 6 times (24 sts).

Rnd 7: sc in each st around.

Sl st in next st. Fasten off.

OUTER EAR (MAKE 2)

With J10/6mm hook and 2 strands of brown yarn held together, make a magic ring, ch 1.

Rnd 1: 6 sc in ring, pull ring closed tight (6 sts).

Rnd 2: 2 sc in each st around. Place marker for beginning of rnd and move marker up as each rnd is completed (12 sts).

Rnd 3: *sc in next st, 2 sc in next st* 6 times (18 sts).

Rnds 4-7: sc in each st around. Fasten off.

INNER EAR (MAKE 2)

With H8/5mm hook and a single strand of tan yarn, ch 4.

Note: A chain 1 at the beginning of a row is for turning your work and does not count as a stitch.

Row 1: 2 sc in 2nd chain from hook, sc in next st, 2 sc in next st (5 sts).

Row 2: ch 1, turn, 2 sc in next st, sc in next 3 sts, 2 sc in next st (7 sts).

Rows 3-4: ch 1, turn, sc in each st across.

Rnd 5: ch 1, do not turn, continue working forward and sc in each st along curved edge. Fasten off.

EYE RIM (MAKE 2)

With H8/5mm crochet hook and a single strand of tan yarn, make a magic ring, ch 1.

Rnd 1: 10 sc in ring, pull ring almost tight (10 sts).

Sl st in next st. Fasten off.

ASSEMBLY

Stretch Ribbing open wide and insert Head Cover, right sides together, so that open edge of Head Cover meets edge of Ribbing that has the tan patch. Adjust so that center back of Head Cover meets seam of Ribbing. Pin in place, stretching Ribbing open and easing edge of Head Cover evenly around. Whip Stitch together with invisible thread. Weave in yarn ends.

Flatten Outer Ears and sew Inner Ears in place with invisible thread. Sew Ears to Head Cover.

Attach bear nose to tip of Snout. Mark position of Snout on Head Cover with circle template (see Page 98). Stuff Snout and sew in place.

Insert stem of animal eyes through center of Eye Rims then into Head Cover and attach; or cut off stem, glue eye to Rim and sew in place (see Page 8).

LINING

See Page 16 for how to make and attach the foam lining. This will provide structure for the Head Cover and more protection for the golf club. ♦

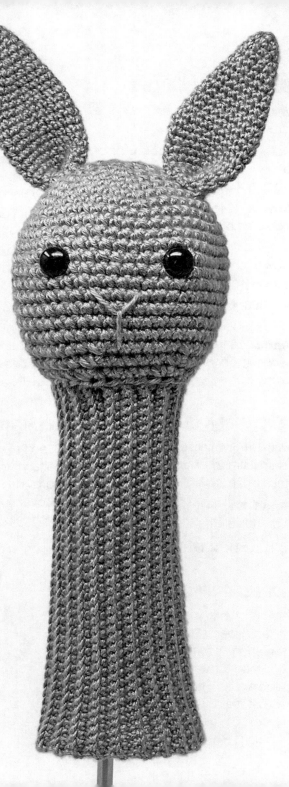

RABBIT

SUPPLIES

Worsted weight yarn in tan 265 yds plus small amount of pink

H8/5mm and J10/6mm crochet hooks or size needed to obtain gauge

Sew-in foam stabilizer, 10" x 20"

Invisible thread & sewing needle

2 black animal eyes, 18mm

Stitch marker

Yarn needle

GAUGE

Be sure to check your gauge (see Page 18) so that the cover is sized as intended and the lining fits.

HEAD COVER

With J10/6mm hook and 2 strands of tan yarn held together, make a magic ring, ch 1.

Rnd 1: 6 sc in ring, pull ring closed tight (6 sts).

Rnd 2: 2 sc in each st around. Place marker for beginning of rnd and move marker up as each rnd is completed (12 sts).

Rnd 3: *sc in next st, 2 sc in next st* 6 times (18 sts).

Rnd 4: *sc in next 2 sts, 2 sc in next st* 6 times (24 sts).

Rnd 5: *sc in next 3 sts, 2 sc in next st* 6 times (30 sts).

Rnd 6: *sc in next 4 sts, 2 sc in next st* 6 times (36 sts).

Rnd 7: *sc in next 5 sts, 2 sc in next st* 6 times (42 sts).

Rnd 8: *sc in next 6 sts, 2 sc in next st* 6 times (48 sts).

Rnds 9-19: sc in each st around.

Rnd 20: *sc in next 6 sts, sc2tog* 6 times (42 sts).

Rnd 21: *sc in next 5 sts, sc2tog* 6 times (36 sts).

Rnd 22: *sc in next 4 sts, sc2tog* 6 times (30 sts).

Fasten off.

RIBBING

With H8/5mm crochet hook and a single strand of tan yarn, ch 41 loosely.

Note: A chain 1 at the beginning of a row is for turning your work and does not count as a stitch.

Work all rows in **back loops only** (see Page 13).

Row 1: sc in 2nd ch from hook and in each remaining ch across (40 sts).

Rows 2-42: ch 1, turn, sc in each st across (40 sts).

Do not fasten off. Pin last row and foundation ch row right sides together. Ch 1, sl st in each st across through both layers to form a tube. Fasten off.

EAR (MAKE 2)

With H8/5mm crochet hook and a single strand of tan yarn, make a magic ring, ch 1.

Rnd 1: 6 sc in ring, pull ring closed tight (6 sts).

Rnd 2: *sc in next st, 2 sc in next st* 3 times (9 sts).

Rnd 3: sc in each st around.

Rnd 4: *sc in next 2 sts, 2 sc in next st* 3 times (12 sts).

Rnd 5: sc in each st around.

Rnd 6: *sc in next 5 sts, 2 sc in next st* 2 times (14 sts).

Rnd 7: sc in each st around.

Rnd 8: *sc in next 6 sts, 2 sc in next st* 2 times (16 sts).

Rnd 9: sc in each st around.

Rnd 10: *sc in next 7 sts, 2 sc in next st* 2 times (18 sts).

Rnd 11: sc in each st around.

Rnd 12: *sc in next 8 sts, 2 sc in next st* 2 times (20 sts).

Rnds 13-14: sc in each st around

Rnd 15: *sc in next 8 sts, sc2tog* 2 times (18 sts).

Rnds 16-21: sc in each st around.

Fasten off.

Flatten Ear as shown in photo below. Use tail to sew both layers together along edge AB. Fold Ear so that A meets B and secure in place with a stitch.

A   B

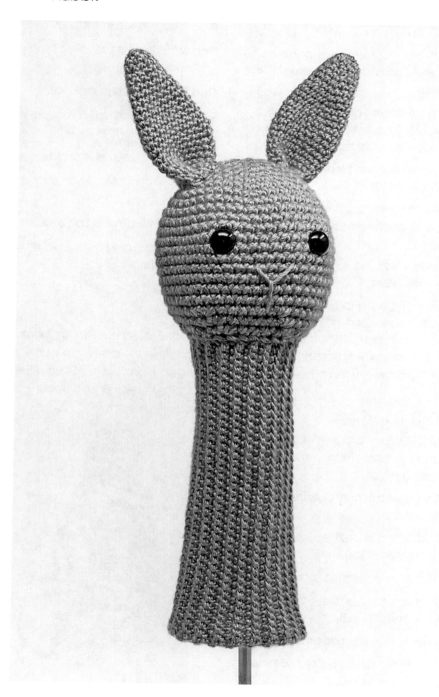

ASSEMBLY

Stretch Ribbing open wide and insert Head Cover, right sides together, so that open edge of Head Cover meets an open end of Ribbing. Adjust so that center back of Head Cover meets seam of Ribbing. Pin in place, stretching Ribbing open and easing edge of Head Cover evenly around. Whip Stitch together with invisible thread. Weave in yarn ends.

Sew Ears to Head Cover. Attach eyes (see Page 8). With a single strand of pink yarn, embroider a "Y" for the nose.

LINING

See Page 16 for how to make and attach the foam lining. This will provide structure for the Head Cover and more protection for the golf club. ♦

IGUANA

SUPPLIES

Worsted weight yarn in green 165 yds and tan 30 yds

H8/5mm and J10/6mm crochet hooks or size needed to obtain gauge

Sew-in foam stabilizer, 10" x 20"

Invisible thread & sewing needle

2 yellow cat eyes, 21mm

2 black buttons, 3/8"

Stitch marker

Yarn needle

Stuffing

GAUGE

Be sure to check your gauge (see Page 18) so that the cover is sized as intended and the lining fits.

HEAD COVER

With J10/6mm hook and 2 strands of green yarn held together, make a magic ring, ch 1.

Rnd 1: 6 sc in ring, pull ring closed tight (6 sts).

Rnd 2: 2 sc in each st around. Place marker for beginning of rnd and move marker up as each rnd is completed (12 sts).

Rnd 3: *sc in next st, 2 sc in next st* 6 times (18 sts).

Rnd 4: *sc in next 2 sts, 2 sc in next st* 6 times (24 sts).

Rnd 5: *sc in next 3 sts, 2 sc in next st* 6 times (30 sts).

Rnd 6: *sc in next 4 sts, 2 sc in next st* 6 times (36 sts).

Rnd 7: *sc in next 5 sts, 2 sc in next st* 6 times (42 sts).

Rnd 8: *sc in next 6 sts, 2 sc in next st* 6 times (48 sts).

Rnds 9-19: sc in each st around.

Rnd 20: *sc in next 6 sts, sc2tog* 6 times (42 sts).

Rnd 21: *sc in next 5 sts, sc2tog* 6 times (36 sts).

Rnd 22: *sc in next 4 sts, sc2tog* 6 times (30 sts).

Fasten off.

RIBBING

With H8/5mm crochet hook and a single strand of green yarn, ch 41 loosely.

Note: A chain 1 at the beginning of a row is for turning your work and does not count as a stitch.

Work all rows in **back loops only** (see Page 13).

Row 1: sc in 2nd ch from hook and in each remaining ch across (40 sts).

Rows 2-42: ch 1, turn, sc in each st across (40 sts).

Do not fasten off. Pin last row and foundation ch row right sides together. Ch 1, sl st in each st across through both layers to form a tube. Fasten off.

OUTER EYE (MAKE 2)

With H8/5mm hook and a single strand of green yarn, make a magic ring, ch 1.

Rnd 1: 6 sc in ring, pull ring closed almost tight (6 sts).

Rnd 2: 2 sc in each st around. Place marker for beginning of rnd and move marker up as each rnd is completed (12 sts).

Rnd 3: *sc in next st, 2 sc in next st* 6 times (18 sts).

Rnds 4-5: sc in each st around. Fasten off.

EYELID (MAKE 2)

With H8/5mm hook and a single strand of green yarn, ch 2.

Row 1: 3 sc in 2nd ch from hook.

Row 2: ch 1, turn, 2 sc in next 3 sts (6 sts).

Row 3: ch 1, turn, *sc in next st, 2 sc in next st* 3 times (9 sts).

Row 4: ch 1, turn, *sc in next 2 sts, 2 sc in next st* 3 times (12 sts).

Row 5: ch 1, turn, *sc in next 3 sts, 2 sc in next st* 3 times (15 sts).

Row 6: ch 1, do not turn, sc in each st across straight side.

Fasten off. Weave in ends.

SPINE (MAKE 8)

With H8/5mm hook and a single strand of tan yarn, make a magic ring, ch 1.

Rnd 1: 5 sc in ring, pull ring closed tight (5 sts).

Rnd 2: sc in each st around. Place marker for beginning of rnd and move marker up as each rnd is completed (5 sts).

Rnd 3: sc in next 4 sts, 2 sc in next st (6 sts).

Rnd 4: sc in each st around.

Rnd 5: *sc in next 2 sts, 2 sc in next st* 2 times (8 sts).

Rnd 6: sc in each st around.

Rnd 7: *sc in next 3 sts, 2 sc in next st* 2 times (10 sts).

Sl st in next st. Fasten off. Stuff yarn tails inside.

SMALL SCALE (MAKE 2)

With H8/5mm hook and a single strand of tan yarn, make a magic ring, ch 1.

Rnd 1: 6 sc in ring, pull ring closed tight (6 sts).

Rnd 2: 2 sc in each st around. Place marker for beginning of rnd (12 sts).

Sl st in next st. Fasten off.

MEDIUM SCALE (MAKE 2)

With H8/5mm hook and a single strand of tan yarn, make a magic ring, ch 1.

Rnd 1: 6 sc in ring, pull ring closed tight (6 sts).

Rnd 2: 2 sc in each st around. Place marker for beginning of rnd and move marker up as each rnd is completed (12 sts).

Rnd 3: *sc in next st, 2 sc in next st* 6 times (18 sts).

Sl st in next st. Fasten off.

LARGE SCALE (MAKE 2)

With H8/5mm hook and a single strand of tan yarn, make a magic ring, ch 1.

Rnd 1: 6 sc in ring, pull ring closed tight (6 sts).

Rnd 2: 2 sc in each st around. Place marker for beginning of rnd and move marker up as each rnd is completed (12 sts).

Rnd 3: *sc in next st, 2 sc in next st* 6 times (18 sts).

Rnd 4: *2 sc in next st, sc in next 2 sts* 6 times (24 sts).

Sl st in next st. Fasten off.

ASSEMBLY

Stretch Ribbing open wide and insert Head Cover, right sides together, so that open edge of Head Cover meets an open end of Ribbing. Adjust so that center back of Head Cover meets seam of Ribbing. Pin in place, stretching Ribbing open and easing edge of Head Cover evenly around. Whip Stitch together with invisible thread. Weave in yarn ends.

Push a small bit of stuffing into each Spine with the eraser end of a new pencil. Thread a needle with tan yarn and string it through the bottom of each Spine to make a row (see photo below).

Sew yarn tails from each end of row up and down through the adjacent Spine to secure the row. Finger-press Head Cover to make a crease from center front to center back. Pin to temporarily hold crease in place. Sew Spines along crease with invisible thread, starting at top and extending down back.

Attach animal eyes to center of Outer Eyes (see Page 8). Mark position of Outer Eyes on Head Cover with circle template (see Page 98). Stuff Outer Eyes and sew in place. Place Eyelids so that straight side slants across Eyes slightly downward toward center front and sew in position.

Sew on buttons for nostrils or make embroidered nostrils from French Knots using a double strand of black yarn.

Sew a Scale of each size to sides of Head Cover.

LINING

See Page 16 for how to make and attach the foam lining. This will provide structure for the Head Cover and more protection for the golf club. ♦

BEE

SUPPLIES

Worsted weight yarn in black 180 yds and yellow 75 yds

H8/5mm and J10/6mm crochet hooks or size needed to obtain gauge

Sew-in foam stabilizer, 10" x 20"

Invisible thread & sewing needle

2 white animal eyes, 15mm

Stitch marker

Yarn needle

Stuffing

GAUGE

Be sure to check your gauge (see Page 18) so that the cover is sized as intended and the lining fits.

HEAD COVER

The Head Cover is made by alternating 2 rnds of black with 2 rnds of yellow. **Change to alternate color in last st of every other rnd.**

With J10/6mm hook and 2 strands of black yarn held together, make a magic ring, ch 1.

Rnd 1: 6 sc in ring, pull ring closed tight (6 sts).

Rnd 2: 2 sc in each st around. Place marker for beginning of rnd and move marker up as each rnd is completed (12 sts).

Rnd 3: *sc in next st, 2 sc in next st* 6 times (18 sts).

Rnd 4: *sc in next 2 sts, 2 sc in next st* 6 times (24 sts).

Rnd 5: *sc in next 3 sts, 2 sc in next st* 6 times (30 sts).

Rnd 6: *sc in next 4 sts, 2 sc in next st* 6 times (36 sts).

Rnd 7: *sc in next 5 sts, 2 sc in next st* 6 times (42 sts).

Rnd 8: *sc in next 6 sts, 2 sc in next st* 6 times (48 sts).

Rnds 9-19: sc in each st around.

Rnd 20: *sc in next 6 sts, sc2tog* 6 times (42 sts).

Rnd 21: *sc in next 5 sts, sc2tog* 6 times (36 sts).

Rnd 22: *sc in next 4 sts, sc2tog* 6 times (30 sts).

Fasten off.

RIBBING

With H8/5mm crochet hook and a single strand of black yarn, ch 41 loosely.

Note: A chain 1 at the beginning of a row is for turning your work and does not count as a stitch.

Work all rows in **back loops only** (see Page 13).

Row 1: sc in 2nd ch from hook and in each remaining ch across (40 sts).

Rows 2-42: ch 1, turn, sc in each st across (40 sts).

Do not fasten off. Pin last row and foundation ch row right sides together. Ch 1, sl st in each st across through both layers to form a tube. Fasten off.

HEAD

With H8/5mm hook and 2 strands of black yarn held together, make a magic ring, ch 1.

Rnd 1: 6 sc in ring, pull ring closed tight (6 sts).

Rnd 2: 2 sc in each st around. Place marker for beginning of rnd and move marker up as each rnd is completed (12 sts).

Rnd 3: *sc in next st, 2 sc in next st* 6 times (18 sts).

Rnd 4: *sc in next 2 sts, 2 sc in next st* 6 times (24 sts).

Rnds 5-7: sc in each st around.

Sl st in next st. Fasten off.

ANTENNA (MAKE 2)

With H8/5mm hook and 2 strands of black yarn held together, ch 10 tightly. Fasten off. Cut yarn close to knot at one end.

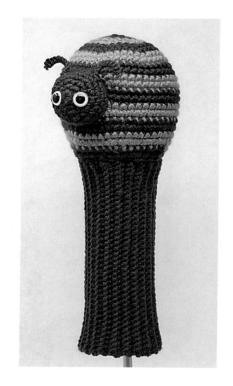

ASSEMBLY

Stretch Ribbing open wide and insert Head Cover, right sides together, so that open edge of Head Cover meets an open end of Ribbing. Adjust so that center back of Head Cover meets seam of Ribbing. Pin in place, stretching Ribbing open and easing edge of Head Cover evenly around. Whip Stitch together with invisible thread. Weave in yarn ends.

Attach animal eyes to Head (see Page 8). Pull long tails from Antennae through Head to wrong side and knot tails together. If you would like to stiffen the antennae, run a needle and thread up and down through the center several times.

Mark position of Head on Head Cover with circle template (see Page 98). Stuff Head and sew in place.

LINING

See Page 16 for how to make and attach the foam lining. This will provide structure for the Head Cover and more protection for the golf club. ♦

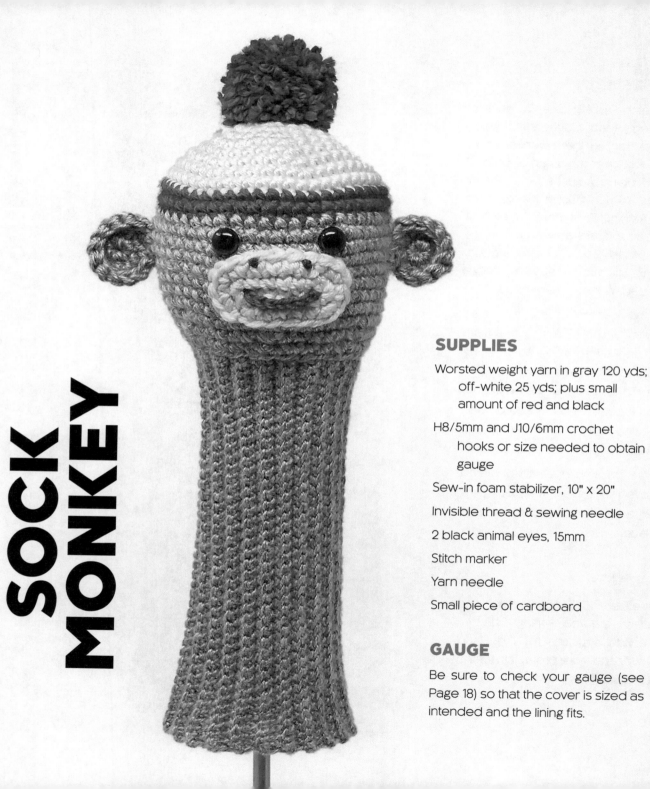

SOCK MONKEY

SUPPLIES

Worsted weight yarn in gray 120 yds; off-white 25 yds; plus small amount of red and black

H8/5mm and J10/6mm crochet hooks or size needed to obtain gauge

Sew-in foam stabilizer, 10" x 20"

Invisible thread & sewing needle

2 black animal eyes, 15mm

Stitch marker

Yarn needle

Small piece of cardboard

GAUGE

Be sure to check your gauge (see Page 18) so that the cover is sized as intended and the lining fits.

HEAD COVER

With J10/6mm hook and 2 strands of off-white yarn held together, make a magic ring, ch 1.

Rnd 1: 6 sc in ring, pull ring closed tight (6 sts).

Rnd 2: 2 sc in each st around. Place marker for beginning of rnd and move marker up as each rnd is completed (12 sts).

Rnd 3: *sc in next st, 2 sc in next st* 6 times (18 sts).

Rnd 4: *sc in next 2 sts, 2 sc in next st* 6 times (24 sts).

Rnd 5: *sc in next 3 sts, 2 sc in next st* 6 times (30 sts).

Rnd 6: *sc in next 4 sts, 2 sc in next st* 6 times (36 sts).

Rnd 7: *sc in next 5 sts, 2 sc in next st* 6 times (42 sts).

Rnd 8: *sc in next 6 sts, 2 sc in next st* 6 times (48 sts).

Rnd 9: sc in each st around; change to red in last st (48 sts).

Rnds 10-11: sc in each st around; change to gray in last st (48 sts).

Rnds 12-19: sc in each st around (48 sts).

Rnd 20: *sc in next 6 sts, sc2tog* 6 times (42 sts).

Rnd 21: *sc in next 5 sts, sc2tog* 6 times (36 sts).

Rnd 22: *sc in next 4 sts, sc2tog* 6 times (30 sts).

Fasten off.

RIBBING

With H8/5mm crochet hook and a single strand of gray yarn, ch 41 loosely.

Note: A chain 1 at the beginning of a row is for turning your work and does not count as a stitch.

Work all rows in **back loops only** (see Page 13).

Row 1: sc in 2nd ch from hook and in each remaining ch across (40 sts).

Rows 2-42: ch 1, turn, sc in each st across (40 sts).

Do not fasten off. Pin last row and foundation ch row right sides together. Ch 1, sl st in each st across through both layers to form a tube. Fasten off.

EAR (MAKE 2)

With J10/6mm hook and 2 strands of gray yarn held together, make a magic ring, ch 1.

Rnd 1: 6 sc in ring, pull ring closed tight (6 sts).

Rnd 2: 2 sc in each st around. Place marker for beginning of rnd and move marker up as each rnd is completed (12 sts).

Rnd 3: sc in each st around.

Fasten off.

SNOUT

The Snout is worked around a foundation chain.

With J10/6mm hook and 2 strands of off-white yarn held together, ch 7 loosely.

Rnd 1: starting in 2nd ch from hook *sc in next 5 sts, 3 sc in next st* 2 times. Place marker for beginning of rnd and move marker up as each rnd is completed (16 sts).

Rnd 2: *sc in next 5 sts, 2 sc in next 3 sts* 2 times (22 sts).

Sl st in next st. Fasten off.

POM POM

Cut a rectangle of cardboard measuring 2" x 6". Wrap red yarn widthwise around cardboard 75 times. Carefully slide yarn off cardboard.

Using a scrap of yarn, tie bundle together tightly around the middle. Cut loops open. Fluff Pom Pom and trim ends into a nice round shape.

ASSEMBLY

Stretch Ribbing open wide and insert Head Cover, right sides together, so that open edge of Head Cover meets an open end of Ribbing. Adjust so that center back of Head Cover meets seam of Ribbing. Pin in place, stretching Ribbing open and easing edge of Head Cover evenly around. Whip Stitch together with invisible thread.

With black yarn, embroider 2 French Knots (see Page 15) at top of Snout for nostrils. Sew Snout and Ears in place.

Attach eyes (see Page 8).

For mouth, use H8/5mm hook and a single strand of red yarn to make a chain 1 1/2" long. Pull tails through Snout to wrong side of Head Cover and knot ends together. Sew across mouth with needle and thread to hold in place.

Tie Pom Pom on top. Weave in yarn ends.

LINING

See Page 16 for how to make and attach the foam lining. This will provide structure for the Head Cover and more protection for the golf club. ◆

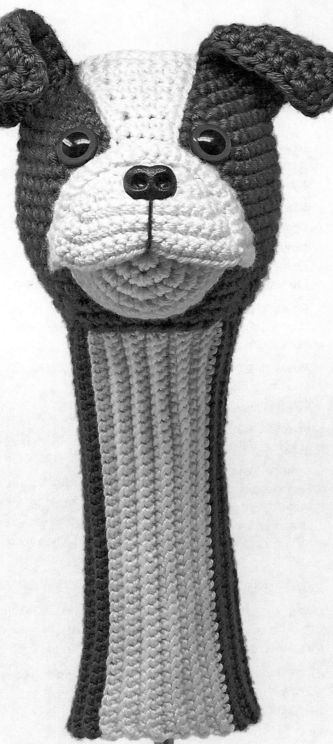

BULLDOG

SUPPLIES

Worsted weight yarn in brown 235 yds; white 80 yds; plus small amount of black

H8/5mm and J10/6mm crochet hooks or size needed to obtain gauge

Sew-in foam stabilizer, 10" x 20"

Invisible thread & sewing needle

2 brown animal eyes, 20mm

Black animal bear nose, 25mm

Stitch marker

Yarn needle

Stuffing

GAUGE

Be sure to check your gauge (see Page 18) so that the cover is sized as intended and the lining fits.

HEAD COVER

With J10/6mm hook and 2 strands of brown yarn held together, make a magic ring, ch 1.

Rnd 1: 6 sc in ring, pull ring closed tight (6 sts).

Rnd 2: 2 sc in each st around. Place marker for beginning of rnd and move marker up as each rnd is completed (12 sts).

Rnd 3: *sc in next st, 2 sc in next st* 6 times (18 sts).

Rnd 4: *sc in next 2 sts, 2 sc in next st* 6 times (24 sts).

Rnd 5: *sc in next 3 sts, 2 sc in next st* 6 times (30 sts).

Rnd 6: *sc in next 4 sts, 2 sc in next st* 6 times (36 sts).

Rnd 7: *sc in next 5 sts, 2 sc in next st* 6 times (42 sts).

Rnd 8: *sc in next 6 sts, 2 sc in next st* 6 times (48 sts).

Rnds 9-19: sc in each st around.

Rnd 20: *sc in next 6 sts, sc2tog* 6 times (42 sts).

Rnd 21: *sc in next 5 sts, sc2tog* 6 times (36 sts).

Rnd 22: *sc in next 4 sts, sc2tog* 6 times (30 sts).

Fasten off.

RIBBING

With H8/5mm crochet hook and a single strand of brown yarn, ch 41 loosely.

Note: A chain 1 at the beginning of a row is for turning your work and does not count as a stitch.

Work all rows in **back loops only** (see Page 13).

Row 1: sc in 2nd ch from hook and in each remaining ch across (40 sts).

Rows 2-15: ch 1, turn, sc in each st across; change to white yarn in last st (40 sts).

Rows 16-27: ch 1, turn, sc in each st across; change to brown yarn in last st (40 sts).

Rows 28-42: ch 1, turn, sc in each st across (40 sts).

Do not fasten off. Pin last row and foundation ch row right sides together. Ch 1, sl st in each st across through both layers to form a tube. Fasten off.

EAR (MAKE 2)

With J10/6mm) crochet hook and 2 strands of brown yarn held together, ch 2.

Note: A chain 1 at the beginning of a row is for turning your work and does not count as a stitch.

Row 1: sc in 2nd ch from hook (1 st).

Row 2: ch 1, turn, 3 sc in next st (3 sts).

Row 3: ch 1, turn, sc in each st across (3 sts).

Row 4: ch 1, turn, 2 sc in next st, sc in next st, 2 sc in next st (5 sts).

Row 5: ch 1, turn, 2 sc in next st, sc in next 3 sts, 2 sc in next st (7 sts).

Rows 6-8: ch 1, turn, sc in each st across (7 sts).

Row 9: ch 1, turn, sc2tog, sc in next 3 sts, sc2tog (5 sts).

Row 10: ch 1, turn, sc in each st across (5 sts).

Row 11: ch 1, turn, sc2tog, sc in next st, sc2tog (3 sts). This row is bottom of Ear.

Rnd 12: ch 1, do not turn, continue working forward and sc along both sides of Ear making 3 sts in same st at tip. Fasten off.

LOWER SNOUT

With J10/6mm hook and 2 strands of white yarn held together, make a magic ring, ch 1.

Rnd 1: 6 sc in ring, pull ring closed tight (6 sts).

Rnd 2: 2 sc in each st around. Place marker for beginning of rnd and move marker up as each rnd is completed (12 sts).

Rnd 3: *sc in next st, 2 sc in next st* 6 times (18 sts).

Rnd 4: *sc in next 2 sts, 2 sc in next st* 6 times (24 sts).

Rnds 5-7: sc in each st around.

Fasten off.

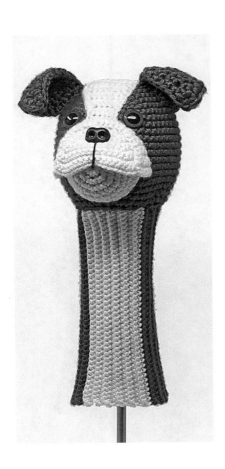

UPPER SNOUT

With H8/5mm crochet hook and a single strand of white yarn, ch 2.

Note: A chain 1 at the beginning of a row is for turning your work and does not count as a stitch.

Row 1: 3 sc in 2nd ch from hook.

Row 2: ch 1, turn, 2 sc in next 3 sts (6 sts).

Row 3: ch 1, turn, *sc in next st, 2 sc in next st* 3 times (9 sts).

Row 4: ch 1, turn, *sc in next 2 sts, 2 sc in next st* 3 times (12 sts).

Row 5: ch 1, turn, *sc in next 3 sts, 2 sc in next st* 3 times (15 sts).

Row 6: ch 1, turn, *sc in next 4 sts, 2 sc in next st* 3 times (18 sts).

Row 7: ch 1, turn, *sc in next 5 sts, 2 sc in next st* 3 times (21 sts).

Row 8: ch 1, turn, *sc in next 6 sts, 2 sc in next st* 3 times (24 sts).

Row 9: ch 1, turn, *sc in next 7 sts, 2 sc in next st* 3 times (27 sts).

Row 10: ch 1, turn, *sc in next 8 sts, 2 sc in next st* 3 times (30 sts).

Row 11: ch 1, turn, *sc in next 9 sts, 2 sc in next st* 3 times (33 sts).

Row 12: ch 1, turn, *sc in next 10 sts, 2 sc in next st* 3 times (36 sts).

Row 13: ch 1, turn, *sc in next 11 sts, 2 sc in next st* 3 times (39 sts).

Row 14: ch 1, turn, *sc in next 12 sts, 2 sc in next st* 3 times (42 sts).

Row 15: ch 1, do not turn, continue working forward and sc along long side. Fasten off.

FACE STRIPE

With H8/5mm crochet hook and a single strand of white yarn, ch 9.

Note: A chain 1 at the beginning of a row is for turning your work and does not count as a stitch.

Row 1: sc in 2nd ch from hook and in each remaining ch across (8 sts).

Rows 2-4: ch 1, turn, sc in each st across (8 sts).

Row 5: ch 1, turn, sc2tog, sc in next 4 sts, sc2tog (6 sts).

Rows 6-8: ch 1, turn, sc in each st across (6 sts).

Row 9: ch 1, turn, sc2tog, sc in next 2 sts, sc2tog (4 sts).

Rows 10-20: ch 1, turn, sc in each st across (4 sts).

Rnd 21: ch 1, do not turn, continue working forward and sc in each st around perimeter of piece making 3 sts in same st at corners. Fasten off.

ASSEMBLY

Stretch Ribbing open wide and insert Head Cover, right sides together, so that open edge of Head Cover meets an open end of Ribbing. Adjust so that center back of Head Cover meets seam of Ribbing. Pin in place, stretching Ribbing open and easing edge of Head Cover evenly around. Whip Stitch together with invisible thread. Weave in yarn ends.

Assemble Snout as follows:

1. Fold long side of Upper Snout forward as shown below and pin in place.

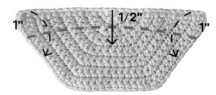

2. Sew along line AB with invisible thread to secure the fold.

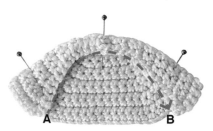

3. Pin Upper Snout to Lower Snout and sew together along back edge (see dotted line below).

4. With black yarn, embroider a long stitch from A to B as shown below. (At Point B, yarn goes into center of Lower Snout.)

5. Attach bear nose.

Sew Face Stripe to Head Cover with invisible thread. Sew on Ears. Mark position of Snout on Head Cover with circle template (see Page 98): Snout will overlap Face Stripe. Stuff Snout and sew in place. Attach eyes (see Page 8).

LINING

See Page 16 for how to make and attach the foam lining. This will provide structure for the Head Cover and more protection for the golf club. ♦

TURTLE

SUPPLIES

Worsted weight yarn in dark green 140 yds; light green 95 yds; and brown 85 yds

H8/5mm and J10/6mm crochet hooks or size needed to obtain gauge

Sew-in foam stabilizer, 10" x 20"

Invisible thread & sewing needle

2 green cat eyes, 12mm

Stitch marker

Yarn needle

Stuffing

GAUGE

Be sure to check your gauge (see Page 18) so that the cover is sized as intended and the lining fits.

HEAD COVER

With J10/6mm hook and 2 strands of dark green yarn held together, make a magic ring, ch 1.

Rnd 1: 6 sc in ring, pull ring closed tight (6 sts).

Rnd 2: 2 sc in each st around. Place marker for beginning of rnd and move marker up as each rnd is completed (12 sts).

Rnd 3: *sc in next st, 2 sc in next st* 6 times (18 sts).

Rnd 4: *sc in next 2 sts, 2 sc in next st* 6 times (24 sts).

Rnd 5: *sc in next 3 sts, 2 sc in next st* 6 times (30 sts).

Rnd 6: *sc in next 4 sts, 2 sc in next st* 6 times (36 sts).

Rnd 7: *sc in next 5 sts, 2 sc in next st* 6 times (42 sts).

Rnd 8: *sc in next 6 sts, 2 sc in next st* 6 times (48 sts).

Rnds 9-16: sc in each st around; change to light green yarn in last st.

Rnd 17: working in **back loops only** (see Page 13), sc in each st around (48 sts).

Rnds 18-19: resume working in both loops, sc in each st around.

Rnd 20: *sc in next 6 sts, sc2tog* 6 times (42 sts).

Rnd 21: *sc in next 5 sts, sc2tog* 6 times (36 sts).

Rnd 22: *sc in next 4 sts, sc2tog* 6 times (30 sts).

Fasten off.

SHELL RIM

To crochet Shell Rim, fold lower portion of Head Cover inward where dark green meets light green (see photo below).

Use J10/6mm hook and 2 strands of dark green yarn held together.

Attach yarn with sc at center back of Head Cover in an unworked front loop of Rnd 17 (counts as 1st st of Rnd 1).

Rnd 1: *sc in next 7 sts, 2 sc in next st* 6 times. Place marker for beginning of rnd and move marker up as each rnd is completed (54 sts).

Rnd 2: *sc in next 8 sts, 2 sc in next st* 6 times (60 sts).

Rnd 3: *sc in next 9 sts, 2 sc in next st* 6 times (66 sts).

Rnd 4: sc in each st around (66 sts).

Sl st in next st. Fasten off.

RIBBING

With H8/5mm crochet hook and a single strand of brown yarn, ch 41 loosely.

Note: A chain 1 at the beginning of a row is for turning your work and does not count as a stitch.

Work all rows in **back loops only** (see Page 13).

Row 1: sc in 2nd ch from hook and in each remaining ch across (40 sts).

Rows 2-42: ch 1, turn, sc in each st across (40 sts).

Do not fasten off. Pin last row and foundation ch row right sides together. Ch 1, sl st in each st across through both layers to form a tube. Fasten off.

HEXAGON (MAKE 5)

With H8/5mm hook and a single strand of dark green yarn, make a magic ring, ch 1.

Rnd 1: 6 sc in ring, pull ring closed tight (6 sts).

Rnd 2: 2 sc in each st around. Place marker for beginning of rnd and move marker up as each rnd is completed (12 sts).

Rnd 3: *sc in next st, 3 sc in next st* 6 times; change to light green yarn in last st (24 sts).

Rnd 4: sc in each st around.

Rnd 5: sc in next 2 sts, 3 sc in next st, *sc in next 3 sts, 3 sc in next st* 5 times, sc in next st (36 sts).

Sl st in next st. Fasten off.

HEAD

With H8/5mm hook and a single strand of light green yarn, make a magic ring, ch 1.

Rnd 1: 6 sc in ring, pull ring closed tight (6 sts).

Rnd 2: 2 sc in each st around. Place marker for beginning of rnd and move marker up as each rnd is completed (12 sts).

Rnd 3: *sc in next st, 2 sc in next st* 6 times (18 sts).

Rnds 4-8: sc in each st around. Fasten off.

TAIL

With H8/5mm hook and a single strand of light green yarn, make a magic ring, ch 1.

Rnd 1: 4 sc in ring, pull ring closed tight (4 sts).

Rnd 2: sc in next 3 sts, 2 sc in next st (5 sts).

Rnd 3: sc in next 4 sts, 2 sc in next st (6 sts).

Rnd 4: sc in next 5 sts, 2 sc in next st (7 sts).

Rnd 5: sc in next 6 sts, 2 sc in next st (8 sts).

Rnd 6: sc in next 7 sts, 2 sc in next st (9 sts).

Rnd 7: sc in next 8 sts, 2 sc in next st (10 sts).

Rnd 8: sc in next 9 sts, 2 sc in next st (11 sts).

Rnd 9: sc in next 10 sts, 2 sc in next st (12 sts).

Fasten off.

LEG (MAKE 4)

With H8/5mm hook and a single strand of light green yarn, make a magic ring, ch 1.

Rnd 1: 6 sc in ring, pull ring closed tight (6 sts).

Rnd 2: 2 sc in each st around. Place marker for beginning of rnd and move marker up as each rnd is completed (12 sts).

Rnds 3-7 sc in each st around.

Fasten off.

ASSEMBLY

Stretch Ribbing open wide and insert Head Cover, right sides together, so that open edge of Head Cover meets an open end of Ribbing. Adjust so that center back of Head Cover meets seam of Ribbing. Pin in place, stretching Ribbing open and easing edge of Head Cover evenly around. Whip Stitch together with invisible thread. Weave in yarn ends.

Sew 4 Hexagons around sides of Head Cover and 1 Hexagon on top.

Attach eyes to Head (see Page 8). Stuff Head and Legs then sew in place, just under Shell Rim. Flatten Tail and sew to Head Cover, just under Shell Rim.

LINING

See Page 16 for how to make and attach the foam lining. This will provide structure for the Head Cover and more protection for the golf club. ♦

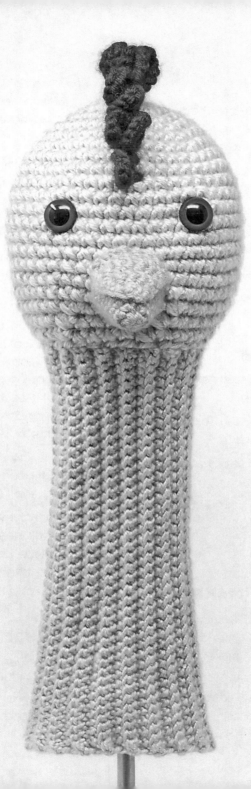

CHICKEN

SUPPLIES

Worsted weight yarn in off-white 230 yds; plus small amount of yellow and dark red (a stiff type of red yarn is best)

H8/5mm and J10/6mm crochet hooks or size needed to obtain gauge

Sew-in foam stabilizer, 10" x 20"

Invisible thread & sewing needle

2 brown animal eyes, 18mm

Stitch marker

Yarn needle

Stuffing

GAUGE

Be sure to check your gauge (see Page 18) so that the cover is sized as intended and the lining fits.

HEAD COVER

With J10/6mm hook and 2 strands of off-white yarn held together, make a magic ring, ch 1.

Rnd 1: 6 sc in ring, pull ring closed tight (6 sts).

Rnd 2: 2 sc in each st around. Place marker for beginning of rnd and move marker up as each rnd is completed (12 sts).

Rnd 3: *sc in next st, 2 sc in next st* 6 times (18 sts).

Rnd 4: *sc in next 2 sts, 2 sc in next st* 6 times (24 sts).

Rnd 5: *sc in next 3 sts, 2 sc in next st* 6 times (30 sts).

Rnd 6: *sc in next 4 sts, 2 sc in next st* 6 times (36 sts).

Rnd 7: *sc in next 5 sts, 2 sc in next st* 6 times (42 sts).

Rnd 8: *sc in next 6 sts, 2 sc in next st* 6 times (48 sts).

Rnds 9-19: sc in each st around.

Rnd 20: *sc in next 6 sts, sc2tog* 6 times (42 sts).

Rnd 21: *sc in next 5 sts, sc2tog* 6 times (36 sts).

Rnd 22: *sc in next 4 sts, sc2tog* 6 times (30 sts).

Fasten off.

RIBBING

With H8/5mm crochet hook and a single strand of off-white yarn, ch 41 loosely.

Note: A chain 1 at the beginning of a row is for turning your work and does not count as a stitch.

Work all rows in **back loops only** (see Page 13).

Row 1: sc in 2nd ch from hook and in each remaining ch across (40 sts).

Rows 2-42: ch 1, turn, sc in each st across (40 sts).

Do not fasten off. Pin last row and foundation ch row right sides together. Ch 1, sl st in each st across through both layers to form a tube. Fasten off.

LOWER BEAK

With H8/5mm hook and a single strand of yellow yarn, make a magic ring, ch 1.

Rnd 1: 6 sc in ring, pull ring closed tight (6 sts).

Rnd 2: *sc in next st, 2 sc in next st* 3 times (9 sts).

Tip: Push with a finger on the center of Rnd 1 to pop the round up to start shaping the cone.

Rnd 3: sc in each st around.

Rnd 4: *sc in next 2 sts, 2 sc in next st* 3 times (12 sts).

Rnd 5: sc in each st around.

Rnd 6: *sc in next 3 sts, 2 sc in next st* 3 times (15 sts).

Rnd 7: sc in each st around.

Rnd 8: *sc in next 4 sts, 2 sc in next st* 3 times (18 sts).

Rnd 9: sc in each st around.

Sl st in next st. Fasten off.

UPPER BEAK

To create this triangular shape, you will decrease 1 st in every row.

With H8/5mm crochet hook and a single strand of yellow yarn, ch 8.

Note: A chain 1 at the beginning of a row is for turning your work and does not count as a stitch.

Row 1: sc in 2nd ch from hook and in each remaining ch across (7 sts).

Row 2: ch 1, turn, skip next st, sc in each remaining st across (6 sts).

Row 3: ch 1, turn, skip next st, sc in each remaining st across (5 sts).

Row 4: ch 1, turn, skip next st, sc in each remaining st across (4 sts).

Row 5: ch 1, turn, skip next st, sc in each remaining st across (3 sts).

Row 6: ch 1, turn, skip next st, sc2tog (1 st).

Rnd 7: do not turn, continue working forward and sc in each st around perimeter of piece making 3 sts in same st at back corners.

Sl st in next st. Fasten off. Weave in ends.

ASSEMBLY

Stretch Ribbing open wide and insert Head Cover, right sides together, so that open edge of Head Cover meets an open end of Ribbing. Adjust so that center back of Head Cover meets seam of Ribbing. Pin in place, stretching Ribbing open and easing edge of Head Cover evenly around. Whip Stitch together with invisible thread.

Make Comb as follows:

Flatten Head Cover and finger-press to create a crease from center front to center back. The Comb is created by working a series of chain loops along the center front crease.

With J10/6mm hook and 2 strands of red yarn held together, fasten on with single crochet (see Page 15) at top of Head Cover (see Figure A).

Row 1: *ch 12, sc in next st* 9 times. Fasten off.

Weave in yarn ends.

Sew Upper Beak to Lower Beak along back edge. Mark position of Beak on Head Cover with circle template (see Page 98). Stuff Beak and sew in place with invisible thread.

Attach eyes (see Page 8).

FIGURE A

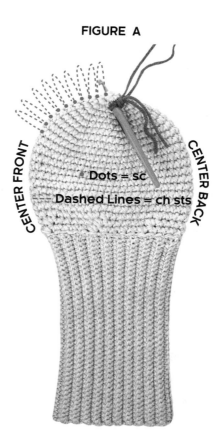

CENTER FRONT

CENTER BACK

Dots = sc

Dashed Lines = ch sts

LINING

See Page 16 for how to make and attach the foam lining. This will provide structure for the Head Cover and more protection for the golf club. ♦

Templates

Trace or copy templates at 100 percent.

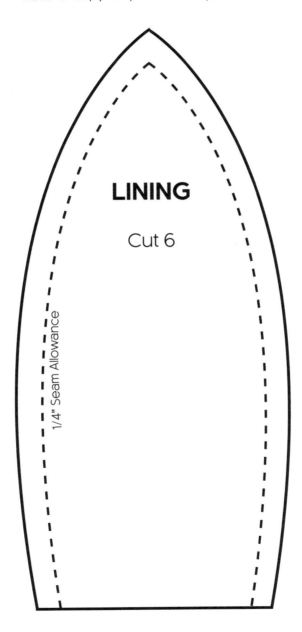

LINING

Cut 6

1/4" Seam Allowance

To mark placement of auxiliary pieces, cut a circle that matches the diameter of your piece and pin in position to golf club cover. Trace with disappearing ink marking pen, tailor's chalk or basting stitches. Remove pattern and pin amigurumi feature over outline to sew in place.

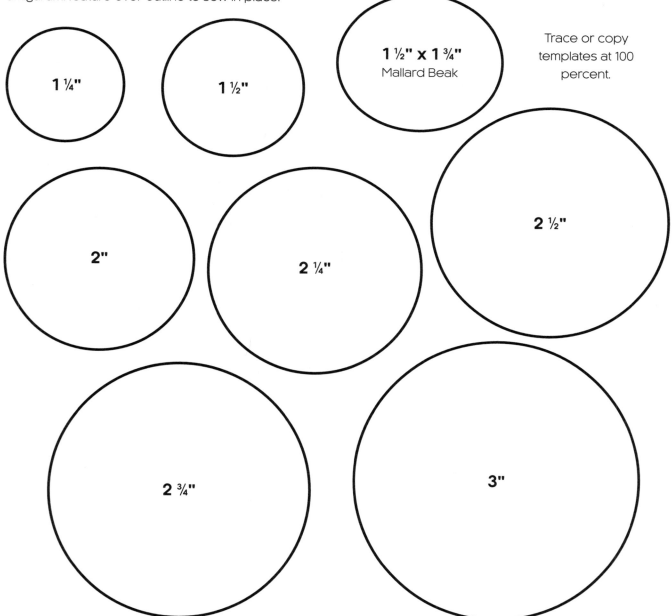

1 ¼"

1 ½"

1 ½" x 1 ¾"
Mallard Beak

Trace or copy templates at 100 percent.

2"

2 ¼"

2 ½"

2 ¾"

3"

Resources

YARN

Herrschners
herrschners.com

Joann Fabric and Craft Stores
joann.com

Amazon
amazon.com

NOTIONS

Joann Fabric and Craft Stores
joann.com

Amazon
amazon.com

ANIMAL EYES & NOSES

CR's Crafts
crscrafts.com

Etsy Shop 6060
etsy.com/shop/6060

Amazon
amazon.com

FOAM STABILIZER

Michaels
michaels.com

Nancy's Notions
nancysnotions.com

Amazon
amazon.com

ByAnnie
byannie.com

VIDEO TUTORIALS

You Tube

youtube.com
Search on the name of the stitch
or technique you want to learn.

Pinterest

pinterest.com/LindalooEnt/
Visit my Pinterest page to view
video tutorials for the stitches
and techniques used in this
book. Look for the board named
"Amigurumi Tutorials".

Suggested Yarn

The following yarns are suggested for making these golf club covers.

Gopher

Lion Brand "Heartland"

    Color: Mammoth Cave, #125

    Color: Grand Canyon, #122

    Color: Black Canyon, #153

Red Heart "Soft"

    Color: White, #4600

Pig

Lion Brand "Heartland"

    Color: Denali, #103

    Color: Sequoia, #126

Alligator

Lion Brand "Heartland"

    Color: Everglades, #173

Red Heart "Soft"

    Color: White, #4600

Tiger

Lion Brand "Heartland"

    Color: Yosemite, #135

    Color: Black Canyon, #153

Red Heart "Soft"

    Color: White, #4600

Raccoon

Lion Brand "Heartland"

    Color: Mount Rainier, #150

    Color: Black Canyon, #153

Red Heart "Soft"

    Color: White, #4600

Owl

Lion Brand "Heartland"

    Color: Big Bend, #124

    Color: Sequoia, #126

    Color: Bryce Canyon, #130

    Color: Black Canyon, #153

Red Heart "Soft"

    Color: White, #4600

Caron "Simply Soft"

    Color: Sunshine, #9776

Lion

Lion Brand "Heartland"

    Color: Great Sand Dunes, #123

    Color: Black Canyon, #153

Red Heart "Soft"

    Color: White, #4600

King Cobra

Lion Brand "Heartland"

    Color: Mammoth Cave, #125

    Color: Grand Canyon, #122

    Color: Denali, #103

    Color: Black Canyon, #153

Frog

Lion Brand "Heartland"

    Color: Everglades, #173

    Color: Black Canyon, #153

Bald Eagle

Lion Brand "Heartland"

    Color: Sequoia, #126

    Color: Black Canyon, #153

Red Heart "Soft"

    Color: White, #4600

Caron "Simply Soft"

    Color: Gold, #9782

Ladybug

Lion Brand "Heartland"

    Color: Redwood, #113

    Color: Black Canyon, #153

Red Heart "Soft"

    Color: White, #4600

Deer
Lion Brand "Heartland"
    Color: Grand Canyon, #122
    Color: Sequoia, #126
Red Heart "Soft"
    Color: White, #4600

Mallard
Lion Brand "Heartland"
    Color: King's Canyon, #180
    Color: Sequoia, #126
    Color: Yellowstone, #158
    Color: Black Canyon, #153
Red Heart "Soft"
    Color: White, #4600

Flamingo
Lion Brand "Heartland"
    Color: Zion, #104
    Color: Black Canyon, #153
Red Heart "Soft"
    Color: White, #4600

Labrador Retriever
Lion Brand "Heartland"
    Color: Great Sand Dunes, #123
    Color: Kenai Fjords, #144
    Color: Black Canyon, #153
    Color: Mount Rainier, #150

Penguin
Lion Brand "Heartland"
    Color: Black Canyon, #153
Red Heart "Soft"
    Color: White, #4600
    Color: Tangerine, #4422

Tabby Cat
Lion Brand "Heartland"
    Color: Mount Rainier, #150
    Color: Katmai, #151
    Color: Denali, #103
Red Heart "Soft"
    Color: White, #4600

Bear
Lion Brand "Heartland"
    Color: Sequoia, #126
    Color: Grand Canyon, #122

Rabbit
Lion Brand "Heartland"
    Color: Grand Canyon, #122
    Color: Denali, #103

Iguana
Lion Brand "Heartland"
    Color: Guadalupe Mtns, #156
    Color: Grand Canyon, #122

Bee
Lion Brand "Heartland"
    Color: Yellowstone, #158
    Color: Black Canyon, #153

Sock Monkey
Lion Brand "Heartland"
    Color: Mount Rainier, #150
    Color: Redwood, #113
    Color: Black Canyon, #153
Red Heart "Soft"
    Color: Off White, #4601

Bulldog
Red Heart "Soft"
    Color: Toast, #1882
    Color: White, #4600
    Color: Black, #4614

Turtle
Lion Brand "Heartland"
    Color: Joshua Tree, #174
    Color: Everglades, #173
    Color: Sequoia, #126

Chicken
Lion Brand "Heartland"
    Color: Acadia, #098
Caron "Simply Soft"
    Color: Gold, #9782
Lion Brand "Vanna's Choice"
    Color: Cranberry, #0180

Other books by Linda Wright

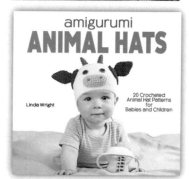

LINDA WRIGHT studied textiles and patternmaking at the Pennsylvania State University. She is the author of various handicraft books including the groundbreaking *Toilet Paper Origami* and its companion book, *Toilet Paper Origami On a Roll*, plus a collection of adult coloring books and numerous works of amigurumi-style crochet. To learn more about these fun-filled books, visit:

amazon.com/author/lindawright   **pinterest.com/LindalooEnt**   **lindaloo.com**

Notes